The Best Police Report Writing Book

With Samples

A.S. Michael

Written for cops by cops, this is not an English lesson!

Visit our website at:

PoliceReportWriting.net

You can:

Compliment our book

Complain about our book

Suggest another book

Order an instant downloadable copy of this book

Link to tell a friend

Look through our in-progress projects

Request a copy for your class

Trumpet Publishing Corp.

1936 Bruce B. Downs #337

Wesley Chapel FL 33543

Publication disclaimer

This book or website or any other publications are not in any way intended to replace or substitute any departmental procedure, state statute, city or county ordinance or federal law or code. Trumpet Publications Corp. , the author and the associate advisors have made all possible efforts to ensure the accuracy and thoroughness of the information and instructional methods, legal references provided herein. Trumpet Publications accepts no liability whatsoever for injury, legal action or any other type of adverse results for following the methods involved in this publication.

The Best Police Report Writing Book, With Samples

ISBN # 1441415033

First printing

2008

Cover Design by Trumpet Publishing Corp.

Logo Design by Erin Clark

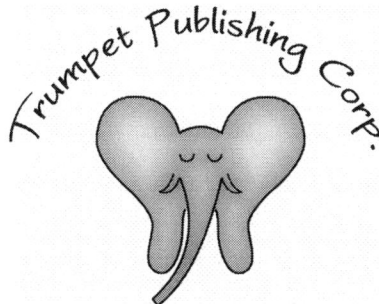

Table of Contents

About the Author

A.S. Michael is a seasoned, veteran police officer and an established, published author. A.S. Michael has been a CJSTC certified instructor of police topics since 1990.

Experience and topics taught include, high liability Defensive Tactics and numerous, extremely dull administrative topics. Administrative topics include Report writing, use of force report writing, pursuit radio procedures, map reading and orientation.

The students have ranged from college level, academy students, to civilian personnel. Also, certified as a field training officer, Michael took new police officers from the academy, and trained them to become fully functioning police officers on the street.

Forums include in-class instructions for several years, and on-line degree courses.

Michael's previous publications and instructional videos sell on a worldwide market, thanks to the advance of the internet.

A.S. Michael is proudly a member of ILEETA

Introduction

Many years ago I was sitting right where you are now, in an academy class, lost. My academy, for the most part was great training. We had very impressive instructors. Our instructors were chosen because they wanted to teach and for their proficiency in training the academy officers. Being an academy instructor was quite the mark in your personnel file. Training did usually lead to bigger and better things, regarding promotions within our department.

Then I took a report writing class. What a difference in teaching methods. Academy training was usually very concise and specific to the subject matter, with great detail and a well rounded instructor knowledge of the subject. However, report writing is a completely different subject. Not only is it a difficult subject to learn, it is an extremely difficult subject to teach.

My report writing instructor was a very nice, much older member of our police department. Very pleasant personality, he was well liked by everyone. He was also the Assistant Chief of Police. So, no one had the guts to tell him his teaching methods stunk. As far as his police experience, in the real world this man had an administrative position. During his entire career, he only wrote police reports for about two years, and that was at the beginning of his career, twenty-five years ago! Depending on an instructor's attention to detail, you can take a report writing class and come out with basic skills. Or, you can come out if it with virtually no skills and still be completely lost. Usually the latter is true.

Then, you are expected to get on the street, learn in real time from your field training officer, adjust per your different sergeants and eventually just figure out how to write a report on your own.

This is the common and accepted method for most agencies. This takes a lot of your time, time you could be using to perfect your interviewing skills. Time you could be using to perfect your investigational skills. For many months you stumble, write and re-write, never coming up with a clear method or pattern to use consistently.

Report writing is a struggle. It is the most common complaint for new officers in the academy and the most common complaint against you from your field training officers. But, this can be alleviated. By having a method or pattern in which to build your foundation of basic report writing skills, you can easily learn to write a police report for any offense. From that basic skill, you will learn to incorporate necessary requirements from others within your agency.

You will learn what elements your prosecutor wants to see for filing and prosecuting a bad guy. You can gain a tremendous amount of confidence knowing any investigation is not above your skill level or reporting level. And yes, all of this you can get from reading this book.

Like I said, I was where you are right now. Report writing is not such a complex thing to learn, but it is very difficult because it is subjective, annoying, tedious and very dull. Your excitement of the day must come to an abrupt stop. You have to sit down, calm down, re-group, focus and try to begin to recall details.

If your offense had you running or fighting your body will be coursing with adrenaline, you will be shaking like a Chihuahua. You will probably be trying to write in your car. If you are handwriting reports you will have a clipboard wedged in the steering wheel. If you're using the computer to write, you will be twisted up trying to reach the keyboard. Oh, and half the time you will be in the dark, or half dark trying to do all this. Welcome to police work!

Chapter 1
Getting Organized

Congratulations to you for your selection of a career in law enforcement. You have just chosen a career that is one of the most fun things you can do while still getting paid, and receiving dental benefits. Get ready to work a great selection of shifts. Free uniforms, a free company car and lots of neat weapons and toys to use against any bad guys that gives you trouble. You will work long hours, wearing heavy equipment, sweating like you never have before, and you can expect to redevelop that little writing callous on your middle finger.

Seriously, police work is the most fun you can have, legally. There will be times in your new career that you will simultaneously love and hate people. You will probably develop strong feelings for your friends in police work and begin to mistrust regular people. Sick stuff makes us laugh. This is all a pretty normal expectation in the basic psychology of law enforcement officers. When you spend a lot of time with a tight group that thinks alike, similar habits develop.

Instead of thinking of this as being a negative, use this as a positive influence. Emulate those that impress you, ignore the dumb ones. When you begin to work on the street you will probably be assigned to a field training officer. Field training is not usually given to just any officer. There is a lot of liability attached to the position of "trainer". Certification courses on how to train, must be obtained. But, the ability to document, in great detail the performance, training, problems, corrections and possible discipline and even firing of the probationary officer must be done properly. That probationary officer being so closely scrutinized, graded and documented is you.

You will be expected to start out your field training by being marginally effective. Your academy training was supposed to get you to this point. However, your academy training may not cover it all. Prior to beginning you career in law enforcement, please understand this is potentially a physical job. We run, we jump, we fight, and we fall down. You have to be able to handle all this, keep your cool, defend yourself then sit down and write about the incident in a clear, cohesive, and concise manner.

Come to your first day prepared. Some of you that have grown soft around the middle may need to begin to prepare months in advance. Get yourself in shape. Not only will you be able to perform the job of a police officer, you will have a more authoritative, command presence. Do not show up to do the job as a police officer with any kind of attitude that physical exertion is not your job, getting sweaty is not your thing.

Training officers gossip about you just as much as you gossip about training officers. The tough trainers have a reputation, stories that follow them around. Make no mistake, officers being trained get a reputation very quickly as well.

Trainers know who is smart and has caught on very quickly. Trainers know who is a good prospect, but will need a bit of extra effort. Trainers also know who is useless, cowardly, not catching on and blames everyone else for their deficiencies. You do not want to be the latter. Arrive in shape, study, read and realistically prepare yourself for your new job.

You will not be expected to know everything about everything, but you will be expected to have an open and learning attitude. This attitude will go a long way in determining what type of officer you are. Are you the one who needs, and will get extra help, or the one who is just not worth the effort and will begin to have a "package" put together to get removed?

Getting prepared to do this job is actually quite easy. Your attitude is extremely important. Basic police skills, beginner level knowledge, is what you will have received from your academy training. All that is left is you. Begin, prior to your first day of working on the street by trying all your equipment on.

I know you have probably already had the uniform, hat and gun belt on while you practiced your quick draw in the mirror, yeah we all did it. Put that uniform back on, ballistic vest, gun belt, boots, all of it.

Walk around. Are you comfortable? Beside the fact this stuff is heavy, (averaging 30 pounds) can you breathe? Adjust the vest. Jump up and down. What just happened to the gun belt? Did it shift? Take it off. Re-adjust the equipment. Next, sit in a chair with the gun belt on. Do you have a piece of equipment stabbing you in the kidneys? Move things around, tighten individual pieces with keepers so they do not shift while you run. Twist, move, jump and chase your kids around the backyard. Adjust, re-adjust, fix, and bolt everything into the most comfortable position for you. You will be wearing this stuff for 10 to 12 hours a day. If you are not comfortable you will be fidgeting and you will be constantly distracted. That is potentially dangerous. Get it all comfortable now so you can concentrate on police work your very first day.

Now that the physical police equipment is set just how you want it, let's look at the other administrative type equipment. When you work on the street your first concern is officer safety, yours and your trainer. Practice good safety by having the habit of always having your gun hand empty. When you go on a call you will need to set yourself up with the ability to document information without having to go back to your car for a clipboard and paper. Get a notepad.

Buy a twenty pack of single, spiral, small, lined, cheap notepads. Put one single notepad in your rear, pants pocket. Do not carry any other notepads. Do not stash one in your shirt pocket, that pocket is for pictures of your kids, dog, wife or lipstick. Do not put it in the same pocket as your wallet, it may flip out when you pull your notepad out. One notepad, one pocket this will get you organized immediately, prior to your first call.

I used to give my students notepads to write on in my report writing class. Initially, they thought they were going to sit comfortably and write on a big sheet of blank paper on a nice, spacious desk. Not a chance. My students had to write notes on a notepad, while standing up in the classroom. I gave them a format for taking notes and they began practicing right there, in the classroom. Imagine your comfort level if you already know how to take notes. You already have a practiced format on what order to ask questions and how and where to write these notes in your notepad. Practicing this, you will know where the notes are for every call. Your easy to recognize format for note taking is identical for each call. You know how to find everything quickly and easily to retrieve them and write your police report.

You are getting organized!

Your main goal while in the field training program will be to get yourself self sufficient as quickly as possible. You will not do this by memorizing everything, studying and killing yourself. Or, trying to learn everything in your training materials. You will do this by organizing yourself.

Being organized does not mean you will know all your state statutes, but you will know how to look them up quickly. You will not know all your departmental policies, but you will know where they are and how to reference them fast. You will not memorize the names of people involved in your incidents, but you will be able to scan your notes and find them later. No shuffling through several notepads. No searching through your clipboard for where you scribbled that phone number, just one single, solitary notepad carried in the same place, every time.

My first problem officer I trained was a report writing mess. She was at the level of, "do we fire or do we fix her". She had a great attitude. She was easy to work with, great with victims. Pleasant, but not a pushover. She could get tough if needed, good mommy voice with lots of bass. She even showed good judgment in her actions. I thought she was a keeper but, she needed work with report writing. She was given to me because I was already teaching report writing. This was her only weakness and it was a severe deficiency.

I took her out to get a feel for what was going on with her report writing issues. Our first call, she rode in the passenger seat. I wanted all the pressure off her so I could see her really try to perform. Our call was voice dispatched. She wrote down this information on a large notepad she kept wedged in the dash.

When we arrived at the call she got out, gun hand empty, good officer safety. So far so good. She approached the complainant and began the investigation. Great. After speaking with everyone involved she then began to take down notes. This is where things went bad.

Remember, her first set of notes was back in the car, on the dashboard. Not too terribly important, that notepad had the location, time and type of call. But, it was another source of notes. When she wrote down the complainant's name, she asked all the right questions, in the right order. She put these notes on a small notepad she had in her shirt pocket. Then she put that notepad back in her shirt pocket. However, her next witness' name was written down on another notepad. This notepad came out of her pants pocket. She opened this notepad right in the middle and began writing. She flipped the page over and wrote more notes on the back of this page too. I tried to mentally remember where she was putting all this formation, but I was getting a bit lost just watching.

Then came the time to sit down and write the report. I watched her shuffle through pages and pages of notes. She had three notepads laid out, trying to locate within them her notes for this call. She did not label the victim at all, so this name and the witnesses name were almost transposed. Finally, after about 30 minutes she was completely frustrated, sweating and exhaling at herself. She told me report writing was just so hard! She hadn't even written anything on the report yet.

She put the car in drive and told me she was going to have to go to the sector office to finish this because she needed more room to spread out her notes. Nope. Not going to happen. Police work involves discomfort. You want comfort, get a desk job, you ride with me we stay outside.

I decided to rescue her before she completely defeated herself mentally and shut down on me. I began with letting her know her investigative skills were really very good. She met with, spoke to and obtained all the information needed to complete the call. This calmed her just a bit. Then I let her know what I saw as her biggest problem with investigating that last call. It was not her police work, not her officer safety, not her ability to establish a rapport, but rather it was her organization.

She looked at me like I had three eyeballs. She was totally confused, surprise and had no idea what I meant. No one had ever mentioned organization to her before.

I started by talking her through the call, beginning with the dispatched information she had put onto the spare notepad. Then, we went through the call person by person, play by play. She understood the call clearly, she investigated properly, but just could not retrieve the needed information to even begin to write about it.

We began by pulling the notepad out of her back pocket and rewriting all the notes of this call. She was all over the place, flipping pages, rewriting names, and recalling details. Finally after about an hour, [no I'm not really this patient] she was ready to write a report.

I had her take a deep breath and begin to think about her next step. I had her think about the type of crime we just investigated. Even though the dispatcher gave it to us as a petit theft, was it really a petit theft, after we investigated it thoroughly? Yes it was. What is our first piece of paperwork needed to begin to write a petit theft for our agency? We began with an incident report.

She took out an incident report and looked at the fill in the blank portion. Suddenly she smiled. She just realized I had her rewrite the notes on her notepad in the exact order she would be retrieving them for the report. She continued to smile as she went from space to space writing in information into all the correct spots. She did this neatly, quickly and she finished confidently. She just realized what a set of organized notes looks like.

It was because of her that I added note taking to my report writing classes. It was because of her struggles that I made my students stand in class while practicing note taking. It was because of her, the method or order of taking notes matched the departments fill in the blank portion of the incident report. It was because of students like her I am writing this book.

Chapter 2

Taking the Call

Now that you have passed the academy, set up your equipment, and learned enough to know you don't really know anything, it's time to do some police work.

Normally, most agencies will put you out with a field training officer to continue where your academy training left off. This is exactly what it sounds like. You will be dressed like a real police officer. You will have a gun, with bullets in it. You will be in a police car riding around, taking calls and solving crimes. You have full arrest powers. But, it is still training.

When you leave the station and go out on that first call your agency will usually send the call to you. You could get this call from a dispatcher, reading the information to you over the police radio. Or, you may get the information sent to you via a computer dispatch system. If the call is voice dispatched, write the information down. Use the notepad in your back pocket to do this. You will need the address, complainant's information and why they want the police to come to them. You may not get this much information, but do write down what you get.

Pay Attention to Where you Are

When you arrive at the location of the call try to orient yourself to where you are. Meaning direction.

Which way is north, south and so forth. Make a quick mental note of the weather conditions. Rain, drizzle, dark, just got dark, sun just came up, that type of thing.

You should already know what street you are on, along with the address or hundred block or cross street.

Anyone around? Anyone running away at the sight of the police car?

Pay attention to the location of the crime scene. Is it a field? A dirt field or grassy field? Tall grass or maintained grass?

Are you at a residence? One-story or two? Wood frame, block, brick, single-family home, townhome, attached duplex or condo. Apartment building, trailer park? Business area, industrial, dock, a professional park?

Things to notice when you pull up

- Direction

- Location

- People

- Anything weird

Notice it, file it for later

Which direction does the location face? What streets are along the sides or front or back? Any alleyways, other weird types of access?

Is the area wooded, landscaped, water nearby, interstate ramps, railroads?

Establish

- Who

- When

- Where

- Is it a crime?

Next

- Keep them focused

- Control safety

- Are they comfortable

- Get both sides

What kind of obstructions does the location face? Visible from the street or other populated areas? Easy escape routes for someone running or driving away fast?

These are things you will take in, in a flash of a second when you arrive. Don't stand there and try to write all this down, just be aware of what is around you, in case these types of details become necessary and need to be documented for further investigation and descriptions.

Who to Talk to First

The Interview:

When you are walking up to the call, keep both hands empty. Your first person you need to contact will probably be the person who called for the police. Try to locate them to find out what is going on and where you should start.

This person might even find you. They may come up to you, or wave you down, or be the one bleeding when you arrive. Approach them, if there are obvious injuries or they look sick or distressed, ask if they need an ambulance. This is a liability issue. Don't let an obviously injured person go without medical attention, just so you can conduct an investigation. Attend to medical needs first, if there are any.

No injures? Great ask the person if they called for the police, and ask what happened? When you talk to people, most will be very excited, mad, or hysterical and want immediate results for whatever their complaint is. You are the first person they are talking to and you just might get the brunt of their frustration thrown right into your face. Get used to it. It is not a personal thing, it is just the uniform.

If they are mad, hysterical, upset or drunk, try to calm them down. Asking them what happened gets them thinking. Speak calmly to them, to bring their excitement level down just a bit.

Ask them to walk you through what happened. Have them begin by telling you where they were when the incident first happened, or when they knew something was not right. They will begin to tell you their story of what happened or what they think happened, let them talk.

Establish When

Ask them when this offense happened. Not recent, or not sure exactly when? If they were at work, when did they leave and when did they come home. If they were sleeping, when did they go to bed when did they get up? These types of questions will apply to delayed offenses and help you establish a time frame.

Your report will have a spot to document when an offense occurred and when it was reported. These times showing when an offense occurred and when it was reported can be the same, or hours or even days, months or years different.

Establish Where

Believe it or not, some people will get their car broken into at work, then leave. They drive home 50 miles, across two different jurisdictional boundaries, to report the incident, and want you to respond. Check to make sure the crime is within your jurisdiction. If not, kindly educate them as to how the whole jurisdiction thing works. Don't just refuse and leave, that really annoys people.

Is it really a crime?

Guide them by asking were the bits and pieces of information fit into the statutory guidelines of the offense for your state.

This means, are they really reporting a crime?

Sometimes people will make their complaint of something someone did to them, that is simply not illegal. But, they will tell you, ",,,*that seems like a crime to me*…" Make sure they are giving you enough elements to cover your ability to charge a person with an actual crime, or at least write out a report for a crime.

Keeping Them on Track

Most of the time they will give you the facts completely out of order, have them put things back into chronological order for you. As you ask them information to guide them in this manner, they may begin to recall details better. They may even begin to catch on, and give you the information in a better order. Have them explain the details until you can create a mental picture of what happened.

If they go off on tangents of details, rants of subjects that have nothing to do with nothing, steer them back to the offense. Otherwise, they will use you for their sounding board for all their grievances; you will be trapped there forever.

Controlling the Interview

If your activities are drawing a crowd, walk them away, don't let them get dramatic and draw an even bigger crowd. Some victims love to yell, roll around on the ground and just make fools of themselves trying to show off. Nip this in the bud, separate them from the crowd, onlookers or other nosey people.

Making Them Comfortable

If they become evasive or overly upset or embarrassed by talking to you, walk them away from anyone that can overhear. Take them away from their boyfriend, parents or employer. Do not isolate yourself. Keep your partner in sight but, just out of earshot so no one can hear them telling on them.

Pay attention to the type of victim you have too. If you have a female victim of a sexual battery, she may want a female officer. However, I have seen some sexual battery victim's more comfortable with a man. One victim told me she was more comfortable with a male officer. She felt safe and didn't think a man would be as judgmental towards her. If your victim seems at all reluctant to talk to you, offer them an alternative officer to come in.

Follow your departmental guidelines in interviewing children. There are laws in place for interviewing children who are victims. There are laws in place for interviewing children who are suspects. States are different, departments are different. Make sure you follow yours and document that you did follow the rules in the investigation portion of the report.

Two Sides to Every Story

Some people lie to the police. They will actually tell you something that's not true. They have many reasons for doing this. Sometimes, it is to get a report for insurance money. Sometimes, it is to mislead you and keep them from getting into trouble. And sometimes they lie to get their loved ones taken to jail. It is human nature to believe the first story you hear as being the truth. Healthy skepticism takes a while to develop.

When you take a call and the complainant is giving you their side, always remember, if they are a victim, there is a bad guy somewhere. Try to find that bad guy, interview them and get their side of the story. Look for witnesses to talk to as well. Look for physical evidence at the scene to match up with the different stories, physical evidence does not lie.

Years ago, I was assigned to a domestic violence call. When I got to the home and spoke to the victim, she was bleeding from her mouth, her lip was cut and she had a loose tooth. She told me her drunk, mad husband hit her for no reason. Now, normally the statement, "no reason" raises an alarm. There is usually a reason. But, she was bleeding and she had given me enough probable cause to arrest the husband and take him away.

Then she told me the husband was next door, and I should go arrest him now. I waited for my back up and went next door to talk to, and arrest the husband. He was huge. About 6,5" heavy build. Great. This might not be so easy. I will probably need to convince him into the back seat of my car.

But, his demeanor was kind of off for a supposed drunk, mean guy who hits people for no reason. So, I told him I had just spoken to his wife, and now I wanted to get his side of the story. His story was a bit different.

He said she had come home late and dunk. When he asked her where she had been, she screamed at him and picked up the cordless phone. He tried to take the phone from her hands so they could talk, but she held onto it and snatched it back. They ended up in a back and forth type of pulling match over the phone.

Finally, he just let the phone go. She yanked so hard, she hit herself in the mouth with the phone. Then she threw the phone at him, scratched his face with her fingernails and ran out. The phone missed, and hit the wall, it left a mark on the wall.

The phone was still lying behind the couch where it had originally landed. Dad had some nice scratch marks on his face too.

This story is changing just a bit. But, even better, I had witnesses. This man's two sons were there, and saw the entire thing. I spoke with the two boys outside, where they could not hear each other, and their Dad could not hear them either. Both their stories matched their dad's story exactly, not the stepmom. I even asked the questions a bit out of order. But, they didn't flinch, they had definitely watched this fight unfold.

Guess who went to jail?

Translating their language, slang

Keep in mind, when you meet various victims, witnesses and such, they might not be the brightest people you come into contact with. Some people are from different environments, backgrounds. They have vastly different educational experiences and levels. They may even speak different languages. But still, some are just dumb.

Many people you meet could be combining a lack of sufficient education with years of street language or slang and an extensive amount of fried brain cells, due to drugs or alcohol abuse. These people tend to call a lot, for you to solve their problems. Some do end up as real victims, of real crimes. It is important, when communicating with these victims that you take a bit of extra time to try to communicate effectively.

Depending on the area, you could be encountering an individual who speaks with an accent, limited knowledge of English, or such a limited education that they only know slang to describe their incident. If you have a language barrier, find an officer to translate. You can legally find a bystander or family member to translate as well. You will need to get the personal information of the translator to add to the report as a witness. This explains, later in court how you got the information out of a victim who spoke little or no English.

However, if your victim is someone who communicates using slang, there are a few things to keep in mind when writing out their interview.

Basically, when you interview this person, you may have to say some crazy things and hear some crazy things. You will need to communicate in their language to understand what they are trying to say. You may have to use street language or slang yourself, just to ask basic questions. Their response will be in slang or street language as well.

This little conversation of grunts, screams, slurps and giggles is not what goes on the police report. Even though you needed to dumb down the conversation dramatically to communicate, you will need to smarten up what goes on paper.

For example, when you speak to a complainant and they tell you,

"I was rolled,,,,".

This is a common term for a strong-arm robbery.

Our city's homeless population used to get their monthly social security or SSI checks cashed, and keep the money in their pocket. Then, the homeless guy would sleep on top of the pocket the money was in. The bad guy would forcibly roll them over and take the moey out of their pocket and run off.

When you interview them you may speak in their language to understand what the offense was. Just document the uncommon words as a street term for what happened.

Here is what the report should look like:

Police Report

Interview:

...the victim stated he, " was rolled". A common street term for strong-arm robbery.

When this method becomes vital is when your victim simply cannot describe to you any other term, for the details of a serious offense.

For example, your complainant is the victim of a sexual assault. She is very un-educated and speaks predominately in street slang. She is the victim of a serious crime, she still needs a complete, thorough investigation completed by police. But, when you talk to her, the only words she knows to describe the incident are raw. Very difficult to really know the meaning of, and it is all she is capable of giving you.

Interview her in whatever manner necessary to get the information out of her, take notes as to the exact words she is using to describe what happened to her. And, due to the seriousness of the offense, be prepared to use her exact terminology in the police report you write.

Here is what the report should look like:

Police Report

Interview:

...the victim stated the suspect , " jizzed" on her. A common street term for ejaculation.

You always want to put the victims terms, comments or slang into quotes. Not everything they say, just the important, not so common terms that help to explain the seriousness of the crime they are trying to report.

You want to avoid having anyone reading the report think that you speak in this manner or use these terms. It is fine to communicate in this manner to be able to relate to the various complainants or victims. But you must always smarten up the content for your report.

Talking to a Potential Bad Guy

When you speak to someone who may end up getting arrested, there are a few rules to follow that are very important. If, during the course of an interview, you feel this person may end up getting arrested, go ahead and remind them of their Miranda Rights.

You are not necessarily arresting them, yet. No handcuffs, yet. But, if you think you may want to use any part of what they are telling you against them, read them their rights. If you are conducting the investigation and they are not free to leave, until you are done asking questions you have to do this. It is called a non-custodial interrogation.

Now, this just might shut them up and they refuse to talk to you any more, fine. That is a risk you have to take. But, if they agree to keep talking to you, get all the information you can. If they stop at any time and want a lawyer, you need to stop asking questions. This does not mean we are going to run out and get them a lawyer, no way. We just quit asking them questions. Now, they can just sit and wait for us to decide of we want to arrest them or not.

If you witness the crime and you want to arrest them, like the possession of marijuana report sample, you do not have to read them their rights. And, on those types of offenses I do not. During undercover operations where I witness, or am the victim, I do not interview the bad guy at all. I do not care about his side of his story, or his excuses.

What I want to avoid is having the bad guy create an entire, ridiculous story or even an alibi about what happened, in a police report, that I wrote. In this type of situation, an on-scene arrest I never read them their rights, I'm not talking to them, or asking them anything. It's always fun to hear them yell how I forgot to read them their rights and I have to let them go. Some people watch way too much TV.

Remember, you are never able to give anyone the right to remain silent. They always have that right. You are simply reminding them of their right. Any human, any age, on United States soil has this right, promised to them by the Fifth Amendment of the United States Constitution. But, you probably got all this already, in cop school.

When you write your report, in the interview portion for each person, just document that you advised them of their Miranda rights. If you had an on-scene arrest, with no interview just list in the investigation or details portion what you did. The fact there is no interview will explain things.

Talking to a Witness

When you investigate an offense where you have witnesses that actually saw the bad guy, they may not be victims specifically, but they need to be interviewed just the same.

Witnesses can help you to identify the bad guy, the bad guy's car, and tell you what happened, sometimes in great detail. They will probably be just as excited, but they might not be as mad because they are witnesses with no damages, injuries or monetary loss.

Sometimes the witness is also the victim. They may have a loss or they may just be shaken up a bit from the experience. You will still need to interview them, just like above and document their statement in the interview part if your report. An easy example of this is the sample Armed Robbery report. Here the clerk is technically listed as the second complainant because they are not suffering the loss of the money. The fact that they had the gun shoved in their face is actually a part of the statute to make the offense a robbery, it does not elevate the victim, statutorily speaking, (unless they own the place) they are just a second complainant or witness. We still need them, the State needs them to complain, arrest, prosecute and maybe even testify.

But, we especially need them to help us identify the bad guy.

Pry the details out of them

When you are investigating these types of witnessed offenses, like the armed robbery sample, you will need to get very specific with descriptions.

As far as identification, do not ask the clerk to identify the suspect. This just sounds vague, hard and kind of "cop" technical. Instead, ask approximate questions.

Many times a victim will tell you they don't know. This is not because they are trying to be evasive or stupid. They think you want exact information from them, but they don't think they know it. Help them out a bit.

When you are standing in front of the clerk, ask if the bad guy was taller or shorter than you. Use your hands to narrow down the height. What about his build?

Was he skinny, medium or heavy build? Heavy? Was he heavy fat, or heavy muscular?

An approximate age. Was he in his twenties? Thirties? A teenager? Black, White, Asian or Hispanic?

The basics first

- How tall
- Build
- Age
- Race

Distinguishing Features

- Hair
- Facial Hair
- Right handed
- Tattoo

Odd Features

- Limp
- Accent
- Birthmark
- Teeth

Changeable Features

- Glasses
- Hat
- Mask
- Clothing

Try to get even more detail, ask about facial hair? Did he have any, yes or no? What type of facial hair, beard, moustache, goatee? I had a witness tell me the bad guy had a "kintuky waterfall 'n a big ole dirt squirell on his lipar".

Translation,,,? Long hair, known as a mullet and a moustache, on his lip,,,there. Try to remain professional when receiving information from your witnesses, explosive chuckling is not very cop like of you.

Glasses, sunglasses? Hoodie sweatshirt? Hat, mask? Was the bad guy trying to hide his face at all?

Clothing information. If you have a girl who saw this, they are the best for a good clothing description.

The guys can give you great car information.

If you are getting a good clothing description from your victim or witness, concentrate on pants and shoes. Shirts come off quick, they commonly get tossed as they run. A bit more trouble to take off pants, shoes almost always stay consistent.

Physical details. Right or left handed? Which hand was the gun in? Did he gesture with a certain hand, grab items or use force with a certain hand?

Walk with any limp, or unusual manner? Favor any type of a body part? Speak with an accent? Or impediment? Did he sound halting, slow or oddly too intelligent to be doing this?

Were there any visible body markings? Did he have any tattoos, scars or other funny little marks? If there were scars were they surgical scars or fall down scars? Birthmarks, moles, freckles?

Teeth? Did he have any, did he have them all? Anything unusual about them. Braces?

Yes, I have arrested a car thief who had braces. He jumped out of a stolen car, ran around the corner and up to a group of his friends to mingle, merge and blend. His shirt was found in the bushes. As he ran, he stripped, he practically left a trail of clothing for the police to follow. But, he could not hide those braces.

Identifying a Trend

During the course of the crime, did the bad guy say or do anything weird. Weird to the victim or witness but, weird to you the investigator as well. If this is the victim's first robbery, the entire thing will be weird. But, if you have investigated just a few of these and you have noted a pattern while investigating prior offenses, this one may just match your past investigations.

Did the bad guy jump the counter, like the last robbery? Did the bad guy immediately hit the clerk with the gun and take the money himself? Did the bad guy specifically demand no bait money be given to him? Was everyone forced into the cooler? Is it the same dry cleaning business getting robbed at all their locations? Was the same method of entry used in this burglary, and the last?

These actions all lead to identifying a method a bad guy uses. Known on TV as the M.O., modus operandi. Most criminals get into a habit of how they do things. If they commit a certain crime, and all goes well, they tend to repeat these habits again. They do stay within their comfort level, as far as where they commit crimes too.

Lots of bad guys will be arrested for a robbery of their former employer. If you are investigating a crime of a busy restaurant, ask if the bad guys seemed to know their way around the restaurant. Did they automatically jog around that water stand, not even bumping it? Did they constantly watch the direction of the manager's office? Did they pinpoint the manager out of the entire restaurant of men, all dressed in shirts and ties? All of this points to former employees.

Pull the employees aside, one at a time. Even if the bad guys were wearing masks, their walk, voice or any other mannerism may be familiar to another employee.

Walk Through the Scene

The Investigation:

Talk first, then walk. When you have asked the person everything they know, ask them to walk you through,,, physically walk you through the scene. Have them show you where they were standing or sitting when the offense happened.

When you are walking the person through the crime scene ask them about physical evidence details. Usually, they will want to show you "stuff", broken windows, skid marks, tools left lying around, blood, shell casings, that they have found.

The Investigation

- Talk then walk

- Protect the scene

- Control access

- Note evidence

Protect the Scene

If your offense is something your department considers serious, close off the crime scene with crime scene tape. Use the yellow tape you see on TV all the time. It just needs to be run horizontally, about waist high around what you think is the entire scene. Once the tape is up, it is your private area, no one gets in unless you let them in.

Have this tape over expand into your possible scene, you can always cut the size down later. Use this tape to protect the areas around skid marks, shell casings, blood splatters and the body itself, if that is what you are investigating.

For normal everyday calls you do not need any tape at all, just follow your departmental guidelines for this, your FTO will direct you here as well.

Other important people at your scene

If your scene is particularly unusual, violent, involves famous people or involves police as a victim, you will have company.

The media will show up and camp out. Your members of staff will suddenly appear, and lots of other concerned police officers will come too. None of these people are there to help you, they are just showing up and getting in the way. Make sure the crime scene tape is up fast. Then when the police extra's show up, come into your scene and stomp around, smoke like a brushfire, drop cigarette butts, they get their name on the police report.

Their names will go on what is known as a crime scene log. This logs the people going in, the time, purpose and time they left. When this log shows up, and names start getting written down, the traffic into your crime scene slows down dramatically.

However, there will be some people arriving who are there to help. These people will be detectives, crime scene techs, paramedics and medical examiners.

These people get added to the crime scene log too. They will usually supplement to your report or attach their report to your file for prosecution. But, add their information to your report. As the lead investigator you would need to be very thorough.

Here is a Sample crime Scene Log:

Police Report

Crime Scene Log:

Name	Time in	Reason	Time out
Piece, Warren	2100	Paramedic	2235
Stand, Mike	2107	Media	2108
Easly, Rex	2109	Traffic Detective	2230

Just use a blank supplement report, add the heading of **Crime Scene Log** and attach this original to your completed report when you are done and ready to turn it all in.

Know What You are Looking At

As you notice the skid marks and other pieces of physical evidence, ask the complainant was this like this before? Is this normal? Is this out of place? Is this your screwdriver?

Make sure you can describe what a certain piece of physical evidence looks like. Not necessarily why or how it got there, not even exactly what it is, or what it might be from.

When you are investigating a crime scene, do not assume you know why something looks like it does, or was left lying there, or what marks or injuries are from.

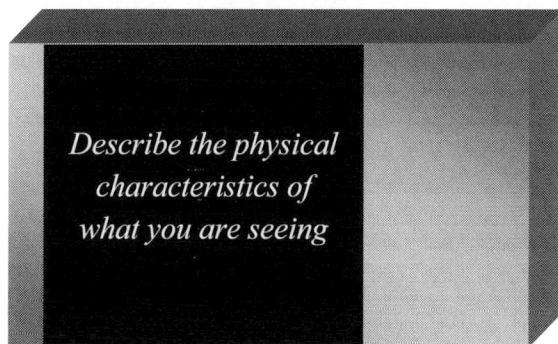

Describe the physical characteristics of what you are seeing

Describing Injuries

If you have a victim telling you specifically that this hole in their chest is from a bullet hole, fine document the hole in their chest is from a bullet hole. This statement will be part of their interview.

But, if the victim is unconscious and the mark looks like it is from a bullet hole, or the victim is dead and it looks like it is from a bullet hole, but it is not from a bullet, you could have a problem

If you document, in your police report that *"**this hole is from a bullet**...."* you will have to testify as to how you knew this. If you assumed something, and you are wrong you could give a bad guy an alibi. You could cause a person to go free, who should be in jail.

Police Report

Investigation:

...a jagged, one inch wide hole in the victim's chest, with a black mark encircling it. The hole has black specs of material encircling it, embedded under the skin.

We just described a common appearance of a close range bullet hole, in a body.

In your investigation, describe and write down what you are looking at, and then stop. No assumptions, no guessing, do not try to help out, just stop.

If it is discovered later, by a medical examiner that the victim was killed by someone stabbing them with a stick, with black soot all over it, fine. Our report still says,

Police Report

Investigation:

I observed a jagged, one inch wide hole in the victim's chest, with a black mark encircling it. The hole has black specs of material encircling it, embedded under the skin.

Describing your Scene

The same principle applies to a basic crime scene too. If your burglary investigation has you looking at an open window, with a footprint on the wall underneath it, just describe what you see, in your investigation.

Do not write this as the point of entry for the burglary.

When a witness comes along later and says the defendant tried to get in the window by putting his foot on the wall and boosting himself up, but kept falling down.

Our report says,

Police Report

Investigation:

I observed an open window with a footprint on the wall underneath it.

A witness could appear and testify in court that,

" after the burglar fell down, the burglar went to the back door of the house. When he turned the knob, the door opened, it was not locked".

We can only testify to the physical markings on the wall. We cannot assume, or we may mess things up and a bad guy gets to go free, from our assumptions.

Now, if you have an actual witness or you, the police officer are the witness to an offense, this changes everything. You, the police officer, saw the bad guy enter through the window, put that in the report. You saw the bad guy shoot the victim in the chest, at close range, put that in the report.

Other than the stuff you actually have a witness for, everything gets its physical characteristics described, and then stop.

What to do with Evidence

Evidence

- Don't touch

- Photograph it

- Measure it

- Dry it

- Unload it

- Catalog it

- Bag it

When you are looking at a piece of physical evidence at a scene, do not touch it. Don't pick it up, look at it, turn it around and show it off. Leave it alone. Post a person by the item, if it is really important or dangerous or valuable. The item should be photographed prior to moving it, or you may destroy the evidentiary value of the item.

Then, the item needs to be collected, preserved for fingerprint processing or other processing. It may need to be dried, if it is wet or blood soaked. Items which may contain particles or hairs need to be handled very carefully so the movement does not lose any fibers. Things such as bed sheets from a sexual battery scene, clothing or undergarments apply here.

Bad guys have been put away for leaving a single hair at a scene that was found, and then retrieved by police. If your scene is important, you will probably have a specially trained crime scene unit to do these things for you. Just be aware of how this process works so you don't touch things you shouldn't. Don't fluff the bed sheets or help the victim mop up the blood soaked floors.

When your scene has been photographed and all items cataloged, photographed and are ready for collection, keep a log of who picked up what item. Again, if the scene is a biggie, your crime scene unit will handle all of this, and simply supplement to your original report. But, if you need to collect that screwdriver at the crime scene, the steps that screwdriver takes needs to be documented.

Document, in the investigation portion of your report that you picked up the screwdriver and you placed it into evidence. That is about it.

This creates what is known as a chain of custody. Be able to state every person who touched the screwdriver from the ground, to the evidence storage, to the lab for processing, the lab worker, back to the lab, from evidence to court here today, back to the evidence storage,,,and on and on, you get the idea.

On a special note, when you are processing these scenes, some of your complainants will ask you about the processing of evidence. I just love these questions.

Here is my disclaimer: As of the writing of this book there is no machine, device, component or other type of equipment that will allow a police officer to drop a bad guy's eyelash into the machine and spit out a full color photo of him with his address, phone number and cats birthday, so quit asking us to use ours.

Chapter 3
Write it up

Have you ever read through your departments guidelines on police report writing? Have you ever read over a set of instructions on how to write a police report only to find you have absolutely no idea what you just read? The instructions left you with no clue what is required, needs to be documented or what the finished report is supposed to look like. I have looked through quite a few police agencies report writing guidelines. They are just crazy. I know how to write a police report and I had no idea what some of these agencies guidelines meant.

To add to the confusion, many of the books you will find on the market today are written by English teachers. Only a handful are written by a police officer. Even fewer are written by a police officer who taught report writing.

Why English teachers just can't cut it

While teaching English or composition writing to students is a viable method for basic skills, it is not the needed format for writing a police report.

You have been here, your English teacher, standing in front of your class is describing how the verbs plurality must match the present participles in the appropriate sentence structure??? OK, that has nothing to do with police report writing.

I have taken a few English composition courses myself, and I have scored well on papers that I have written. However, I recognize there's a huge difference in teaching proper English in a controlled classroom environment, versus teaching someone how to get the dead body, blood stains, shell casings and tire marks from the ground, onto a piece of paper.

The police report writing books available will go into detail about avoiding a run on sentence too. But, if you have ever read a state statute, penal code or any other type of charging instrument or legislation you know this is just not possible.

Why police reports are different

Laws are long winded-dragged- out- get- every- element- and- every- possible- situation- down- in- writing- as- being- bad- illegal- and- simply- not- tolerated- in- our- state- or- else- legal- guidelines.

Of course we are not writing law. But, we are describing an incident, offense or crime scene based on those very laws. We will be required to write in as much detail as possible. We need to document detail to create a picture in the reader's mind, of what the scene looked like. We need to make certain all the elements to prosecute the crime are included in detail, to justify charging someone with the accompanying crime we are describing.

If you fail to document a detail to justify the statute you are charging your bad guy with, he just may get the charges dropped. And you do not get re-arrest him, write another report and try again, you just blew it!

You absolutely have to get the documentation right the first time, every time. No pressure.

Who Reads a Report

-Sergeant

-Detectives

-Supervisor

-Attorneys

-Judges

-Insurance Companies

-Civilians

-News Media

This will not be possible to do within perfect sentence structure guidelines. Now, you cannot write a police report and sound like an illiterate, uneducated moron either, but you are not writing a college thesis.

Always keep in mind who you will be writing the police report for. Your target audience if you will. Who reads a police report? Well, let's explore this.

Who reads the police report

Your first hurdle in writing a police report and turning it in, having it filed and processed as a legal document begins with your sergeant. Once your sergeant reviews and approves your report, your sergeant may be required to turn in the days reports to your desk officer, lieutenant or shift commander. When the report clears this, it will go to your central records section for filing. If no other police investigatory action is needed the report goes into this databank and stored. But, if the case or report needs more work, investigation or follow up, a copy of the report would be shipped to your department's detective unit.

When the sergeants are finished reviewing and the detectives finished detecting if a bad guy is arrested, a copy will go to your prosecutor's office for official filing of criminal charges. When this case goes to trial, all the attorney's will have copies, the judge will have a copy and you should have a copy also.

You will be allowed to use a copy of your report to refresh from while testifying in court. This includes testifying during a deposition, and while testifying on the stand in open court.

In addition to all the official uses for a police report, civilians can get copies as well. Some people will get a copy for mere curiosity. The police report is pubic information. There are certain items in certain types of offenses that are not public information, those are covered in Chapter 5. The media can get copics to re-print details for the news. Public interest groups can get copies too. Anyone, anytime can get a copy for any reason, after they pay the departments copying fee, of course.

You could be writing a police report to document an incident or offense. When you write a report to document an incident, such as a personal accident or traffic accident with damages or injuries, your goal is not to arrest someone, but rather provide the victim of the incident with written documentation of what happened. Their attorney will get a copy of this report to review, and use it as part of a lawsuit to sue someone or something.

Your original documentation at the scene could be invaluable to an insurance company. You cannot imagine how quickly a simple fender bender with no visible injuries, no complaint of pain ends up being a pathetic victim in a wheelchair, neck brace and screaming in pain with the mere idea of an insurance payout.

This is civil stuff, we as law enforcement, do not usually get involved in investigating these types of incidents, but some agencies do as a courtesy, to document injuries. These types of incidents could also include traffic crash reports.

Why we Write Reports

Criminal

- Document an offense

Civil

- Document an accident or injuries

A traffic crash report is usually written on its own state regulated document, with its own strict requirements. But, if the accident involved serious injuries, drunk driving or death the report can become a narrative type report, which this book will still help you to document.

Simple requirements no one tells you about

When you finally finish the investigation and you get to sit down to write your report, make sure you have a few things handy. If you are handwriting the reports, use an ink pen with black ink.

You are legally allowed to use white-out on most police reports. The reports that you write out can have white-out on the originals. Generally, you cannot use white-out if the report form is a carbon-copy type, multi page form. And, you cannot use white-on the form for corrections after it has been turned in. This means passes the sergeant, desk sergeant and submitted for filing. If the report is found to have errors after it passes this hurdle, your corrections will the need to be documented on a supplement type of a report. This is done to safeguard you as well as your agency.

Never, ever do you want your reports to look like you have changed anything inappropriately. Or, made changes after the fact.

Agency to agency differences

When you look at a police report, and you compare them from agency to agency, they all look different. There is no centralized format or style for the format or appearance of a police report. Each agency has had the opportunity, over the years to create their own report style. This style has come from the actual needs of the particular police department. The needs have been created to address the particular state statutes of crimes for each state. The needs have had to address the requirements from the local prosecutor's office as well.

What components make up a police report

But, there is a similarity in content. The similarity is in just three basic components that create a police report.

Those components are, the fill in the blank section, the synopsis section and the narrative section of the police report.

Every police report must contain data from the scene. Data meaning names, locations, times, evidence. This data is usually best documented in a fill in the blank style format. Even though the fill in the blank looks different for each agency, the information collected and filled in is very similar, agency to agency.

Usually on the front of most police reports is a small, narrative type area for a synopsis of the crime. This is a very brief introduction of what the report is all about. It states the elements of the crime and sets the stage for the report you are about to read.

The final portion of the police report is the narrative section of the report. This is the most intimidating, frustrating, annoying, time-consuming portion of writing out any police report.

Components of a Police Report

-Fill in the blank

-Synopsis

-Narrative

Why police reports seem so hard

Because every crime is unique, weird, specialized and different, there is no fill in the blank. There is no drop down menu for the best choice. It is a long, drawn out, old fashioned narrative story of what happened. Told by you.

It is hard to learn, it is hard to get started, it is hard to keep on track and it is very hard to teach. But, there is a very simple method you can use to compartmentalize your investigation into logical sections.

Just break it down

These logical sections run naturally from one to another. They explain your investigation in order, setting you up to then move along to the next part of your investigation to the next, until you have detailed your entire incident. When you are done you will have written out a very detailed, complete, chronological, and easy to read, understand and follow police report.

Since the sections are compartmentalized, you will not have any difficulty in entering details. Nor, will you have a problem recalling details. It works a bit like interviewing the victims and having them answer questions, with a bit of guidance from you, to keep them on track. This method keeps you on track as well as far as organizing your thoughts, prior to putting anything down on paper.

When you read the sample reports in this book, the offenses are all different crimes. But, if you notice after reading a few, they begin to sound alike. That is fine. Having a habit and being consistent when you write out a report is great. This creates a

Organize

- Notes

- Thoughts

- Paperwork

Before you write

format or method for you. You will begin to notice that the details begin to flow better, you recall better and therefore document in greater detail. This will not be immediate. It is not supposed to be. Having you get comfortable with what works for you, and fits your department's guidelines and requirements is the goal.

When you have developed your own method, you will find your investigations actually improve. Instead of agonizing over remembering details, you will begin to look for more. You will know you can document any offense, no matter what is thrown at you.

Fill in the blank

Just about every crime or incident will be documented on an incident report, police report, offense report, whatever your agency calls it. It usually begins with a fill in the blank section.

This is the quick reference section where the most information is contained. A bit tedious, until you get used to the format. Then it is very quick. But, once you have the information completed in the fill in the blank section, you don't have to repeat it again, in the body of the report.

When you are just starting out, take a copy of your agencies report. Take out your notepad and make a few notes. List, in order from your police report, what information comes first.

Meaning, if the location is first, then state statute, then name of crime, then the last name of whomever, put this in your notepad.

Location:
Date: Time:
Crime:
Last name:
Race:
D.O.B.:
Address:
Phone:
Work Address:
Phone:
Role:

This forces you to develop a habit of always asking information in the same order. Then writing down information in the same order. And finally retrieving and filing out the fill in the blank sections in the order information is already laid out on your report.

Starting from the top, let's go over some basics on how to fill in those blanks.

The Title of the Report

U.C.R. Uniform Crime Reporting

The Uniform Crime Reporting (UCR) program was created in 1929 by the International Association of Chiefs of Police to meet a need for reliable, uniform crime statistics for the nation. In 1930 the FBI was given the task of collecting, archiving and publishing those statistics.

Over the years, many chiefs of police departments continued to follow the UCR guidelines to title a police report. What this did for their department, and their city was to re-classify and usually downgrade the severity of a crime.

If these cities routinely classified a report per the UCR guidelines, the FBI statistics showed a lower percentage of Part 1 crimes for that city. Part 1 crimes are the severe, dangerous ones. But, if another city titled a police report by the state statute, this other city a had lot more Part 1 crimes. This last city, although it might have the exact amount and exact type of crimes, looked considerably more crime ridden.

In an effort to make a city look less crime infested, police chiefs are intentionally adopting UCR guidelines to title a police report. There are very impressive news reports of how new chiefs are lowering crime in their city by 30-40%.

It is not technically wrong to do this, but it does appear that the more savvy chiefs are suddenly manipulating this change in their department to make cities look safer, under their command.

What this means for you is, your department may use UCR guidelines to title a police report or they may use state statutes to title a report. You will learn which method, while you are in the police academy. These statistics are a big deal in agencies that are using or adopting them. Make sure your police report is titled appropriately, per whichever method your department uses.

Generally the title of a police report is the name of the crime.

For example, if your department follows statute guidelines and your state statute refers to an employee stealing from the business as either, grand theft or petit theft, (depending on the amount), the crime and title of the report would be:

Grand theft /petit theft are the same, per UCR and considered a Part 1 crime.

However, if your agency follows UCR guidelines, the exact same theft report is titled **embezzlement**.

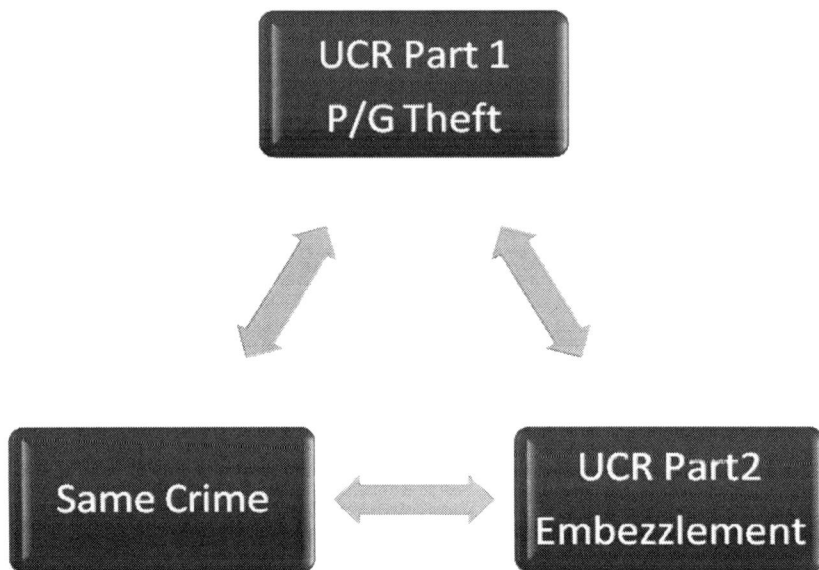

UCR Part 1
P/G Theft

Same Crime ↔ UCR Part2 Embezzlement

Embezzlement is considered, per UCR a Part 2 crime.

See, you made your city safer already.

Where did it happen

Where did the crime, offense or incident occur? When you are standing there, talking to the complainant, they will tell you, they will show you. When you document the location, write in the address. Include the numerical address plus the apartment number or suite or lot number.

Always include North-South-East or West. Don't forget the abbreviation of St., Ave. Ln., Cir.

If you do not designate North-South and so on, you may have two different locations. My city has a 2001 *North* 15th St. It also has a 2001 *South* 15th St. they are about ten blocks away from each other.

If you are investigating an offense at a chain store or a franchise type store, get the store number. This just helps out corporate when you can identify which, of 25 stores in the city. Detectives may need to talk to corporate during the day. One of the first questions is, "which store number?"

Is your location a bit more rural? You can write out the intersection in the blank. Your investigation portion will then go into more detail about the crime scene, which will describe exactly where, within that intersection the crime scene is located.

Police Report

Location of offense: N. Turner Drive and W. Brown Street.

Location reported: N. Turner Drive and W. Brown Street.

Police Report

Investigation:

...the crime scene was approximately 50 yards, directly north-west of the intersection of N. Turner Dr. and W. Brown St.

You can use mile markers on the interstate, just pace out your approximate distance and remember to designate North or Southbound lanes, or East-Westbound lanes.

However, sometimes the location of the offense could be different from the location reported . If someone gets their car broken into at work, drives home to report it and is still within your jurisdiction, you can write the report.

The location of the *offense* was the work address.

The location *reported* will be their home address.

What time did it happen

This blank works like the rest. The time the offense happened might be different then the time it is reported to police, or it might be the same.

The time reported to police is the time the police officer is standing in front of the complainant and has determined that a crime has occurred. It is not the time the complainant called and spoke to a dispatcher.

Normally, most agencies want military time entered here. Unless there is a designation of AM or PM, go with military time.

What day did it happen

Again a repeat from above, the day the offense happened could or could not be different. After midnight is of course, the next date. Even if you work midnights, and the days seem to smush together.

Who is the complainant

There will be spaces to write in who the complainant is. The complainant can be a person, or a business. To determine who goes first, is determined by who has the most damages, injuries, loss or monetary loss.

If you are taking an armed robbery report at a convenience store, and the clerk is un-injured, the first complainant is the business. The business has a monetary loss, therefore the most loss. They get first billing on the report as far as complainants.

You would write in the name of the business. Document the location of the owner, or corporate headquarters under the business address. This is the address where the business lives, and can be contacted during the day, so to speak. The same with the phone number.

Now, if the clerk gets injured, beat up or shot, they get the first listing as the complainant or victim. The business gets listed next, as the second complainant.

When you write in the clerk's information, get their home address and phone number for detectives to follow up. The clerk probably aren't going to be working there much longer, so we need to know how to find them.

But, if business has no loss or damages, they are just the location occurred.

If the victim has simply been injured or damaged in any way, and they happen to be on a business' property, don't list the business as any type of complainant. You will list the location, address and any detailed information, in your investigation. You will not be harming or helping any type of civil case by not listing the business.

Don't allow a victim, who may already be thinking lawsuit, try to tell you the business needs to be listed as a complainant, they don't.

Police Report

Complainant: Bob's Liquor Store # 2311

Complainant: Smith Jr., Robert A.

Any witnesses

Witnesses are confidential information. They will usually be listed on a second page or a location that can easily be blacked out. Always think, how can a dayshift detective find this person? Where is the best phone number for a dayshift detective to locate this person? How can we locate them months from now?

Anyone get arrested

Bad guys getting arrested is public information. This fill in the blank spot is usually right on the front page. Fill in this information, as much as you have.

However, juveniles do not get their arrest information listed as front page, open to the public information. Juveniles arrested are confidential. Unless they have been adjudicated as an adult. But, you probably will not know this at the time of their arrest. Any question here, list them on a back page to keep their identity confidential.

Their name

When you list your complainant, victim or witness, get their full name. By full name, I do mean, Jr. Sr., III and so on. Get their middle initial as well. This will be designated on their driver's license. It should be listed on any police report too. Keeping names consistent helps with identification, agency to agency.

Do they have a nickname, alias or other name they like to use? Get these, list these and document them as A.K.A. (also known as) spare names. They are not legal uses, just another way to identify them or weed them out from the many other John Smith's that are popping up in your computer.

When you try to list a person's name in the fill in the blank part, you might not have a name. This can be due to many factors. Your victim may be deceased and has no identification on them. The victim may be unconscious, in the hospital. The person may pretend they don't know, or they may simply refuse to tell you their name.

Usually, the refusal to tell police their name, comes from bad guys. They may be trying to be difficult. They may have a warrant. Either way, we can still arrest them, we just give them a new name to use, John Doe.

John Doe is a name used, legally for someone who is unknown or is meant to remain anonymous.

In the fill in the blank portion, write in John Doe. They are probably refusing their age too, just write in an estimated age.

When the body, or bad guy is identified, a supplement report would be completed, identifying, giving the real name to the John Doe. But, if your John Doe is going to jail and they still refuse, book them as John Doe. Write this name in the police report, write this name onto your criminal charging instrument. Wanna guess who does not get to leave jail until they can remember their name?

Police Report

Defendant: John Doe

Their address

Your victim, complainant and everyone else's home addresses need to be listed. Even if the offense happened at work, we need to know where to find them, to send detectives to them, serve them, or mail them things.

This information goes under their name on the fill in the blank portion. Complainants go on the front, witnesses go on the back.

In the fill in the blank part of the report, use their local address. But, if they have another address, a second address, or they are part time residents, go to their interview section of the narrative. List the additional addresses there. Follow the same format, to explain what the reader is looking at:

Police Report

Witness: Smith, Margie L.

Address: 1416 N. Magnolia Dr. Indianapolis IN 47345

Police Report

Interview: Witness, Smith, Margie L.

   Additional Address (March-October)

   123 Main St.

      Elsewhere, FL 33602

      The Witness stated she...........

If they are at one girlfriends house this week, and another next week, use any stable relative for an address or phone number.

Also, always ask for their apartment number. Some people just assume we know when they are in an apartment and how to find them. We don't, get their apartment number so we can find them easily.

If you are unable to get the home address from any of your report participants, write in "*at large*" in the fill in the blank section. This can be used for the homeless people who really do not have an address.

But, it is more commonly used for the bad guys who don't want to give us their address or claim they forgot. Fine, we will give them the new address of "*at large'*.

These people get to sit in jail an extra long time too, until their memory improves.

Any property or evidence

Anytime anything is stolen, you will have to list those items. These get itemized, individually and are listed, usually by common name with the brand, make, model and all the serial numbers you can find.

When you are in the complainant's home, usually you will be looking at a clean spot, on the dusty console where the TV, DVD and game system used to be. It may be hard for the complainant to remember what the brand and model were. Remind them all that information was on their users guide when they bought the item. If they can track that down, you will have the make, model, model number, a nice drawing of the item and maybe even a serial number.

If the item is not marked by serial numbers, but rather it is an everyday common item, describe it in detail. If the item is your complainant's cat's Halloween costume, make sure you get the style and size.

When you pick up a piece of evidence from a scene, you will need to describe the item in the blanks. This is where you simply describe the physical characteristics of the item..don't try to say what is used for. Don't assume the red coating on it is blood. If it is evidence you do not need to assign a monetary value.

Just list the item, a craftsman, *"Phillips head screwdriver"*. Any other details will be listed in your investigation. The investigation is where you will write out about the exact location the screwdriver was found. You will describe the red coating, now dried on the handle, that type of detail.

If the evidence item has a make, model, serial number, weight, amount, money count, count of bullets, list all these in the fill in the blank. Where it came from, what it had on it or who had it, will be listed in the investigation of your report.

<u>**Police Report**</u>

<u>Evidence:</u>   1. Phillips head screwdriver

   2. .38 Caliber Smith & Wesson 6" Nickel Plate handgun

   Serial number 132fr7890gb.

   3. (6) .38 caliber bullets from gun

Police Report

<u>Investigation:</u>	...I located a Phillips head screwdriver and a loaded handgun, under the broken window, on the outside of the residence. These items were on the ground, partially concealed from view by planting material.
	The screwdriver had a dried, red substance on the metal tip. The handgun was unloaded and all items were placed into evidence, after being photographed. Digital photos of the evidence are attached to the original report as a separate file.

The only time you may be required to list monetary amount is when you seize drugs. Many states will assign an amount of marijuana, by grams to be either a misdemeanor or felony. List the weight and approximate street value, if your department requires it.

Determine the value

After you describe the item, there will be a spot on the report for value. All you need here is fair market value, that's it.

When you determine the value of an item, you will have had absolutely no training on how to figure out how much the stolen stuff is worth. Many people believe the item's value, they have you list on a police report, is what an insurance company will pay for the item, not so. Insurance companies deflate an item's value to fair market value as well.

If your complainant insists their canary yellow, 1973, 8-track, am/fm stereo, mono-sound player is a collector's item and is worth probably thousands by now,,, look for pricing elsewhere. The best place? Run a quick check on eBay. Check with your local TV repair shops and jewelry shops for similar items.

The reason this is important is there is a monetary difference, in many states for a crime of misdemeanor theft and a felony theft. If you have an item near the amount in your state, making the theft a felony, you should try to get the value as close to correct as possible.

Emotional value is not accounted for either. If your complainant tells you their item is priceless because it was a hand trained parrot that could sing the theme song for CSI Miami. Afraid not. Check with the pet shop, get a fair market value there, and use that on your report.

Many times a complainant will have a check stolen. When you have a blank check stolen, the value is only the price of the individual check. This is about $0.01 each. Even if the check is filled out for an amount and signed, the value is only a penny or two, until the check is cashed.

Once the check is cashed the offense becomes theft for the amount taken. If the bank covers the amount and puts the money back in the complainant's account, which is standard, the victim is now the bank. Your complainant's loss will only be a few pennies for the cost of printing up the check book.

Writing the synopsis

The synopsis, reconstruction, brief or summary is usually located on the front page of your police report. The purpose of the synopsis is to inform the reader of the overview, or facts of the report. This area tells the reader if the report is a basic report, or has arrests, or is something the reader needs to read carefully. It basically lets the reader know, quickly, the information in the report, without reading the entire thing.

When you begin to write out this section, you will notice it is a short space. It is not meant to be long winded, detailed or loaded with numbers, fact or figures.

It is meant to summarize and list the details of your states charging statute. Listing the elements of the crime, in narrative format, to justify the titling of the report.

You will not be required to repeat any information from the fill in the blank sections.

Say you are taking a call for a crime. You have no suspects or witnesses and not much to go on really. The complainant is telling you some of their things are missing from inside their home. And oh yeah! They never lock their doors. This is much easier than it sounds, here is a very basic sample of a synopsis.

<u>Synopsis</u>

An unknown suspect entered the unlocked home, took the listed property, and fled, unseen, in an unknown direction.

This is about as easy as you can get for, some unknown bad guy went into someone's house, none of the doors or windows were locked. The bad guy took some stuff, that is listed in detail in the property section. The bad guy got away and nobody saw a thing.

This is of course, a burglary. Most states require the elements of unlawful entry and the taking, or attempted taking of things. These two elements are needed to justify writing the report, and charging anyone with the crime of burglary.

But, what if a bad guy was seen by a witness?

Synopsis

The suspect entered the unlocked home, through the rear door, took the listed property and fled on foot in a south-west direction.

This describes the same offense, but now you have a witness who saw the bad guy run off.

The contact information for the witness is listed in the witness section, so we do not need their information here. The suspect's information is listed in the suspect's area, so we do not need to list any of it here. The bad guy ran off, and was not caught.

And finally, what if the bad guy is caught and arrested?

Synopsis

The defendant entered the unlocked home. Took the listed property and fled on foot in a south-west direction. The defendant was arrested after a short foot chase with police.

The defendant's name is now known, but we do not need to list it here. The bad guy's information will be listed in the fill in the blank section for arrests.

Who were the arresting officers? They will be listed on the bottom of the report in the officers section, or on their own supplement report.

What was the address? When did this happen? All listed in the fill in the blank portion of the report.

What are the details of the foot chase? This will be listed in the investigation section of the report.

How do we know the defendant went in through an unlocked door? The witness saw him. Want more details on this? Read the witnesses interview in the interview section.

What happened to the stuff the bad guy stole and ran off with? Read about it in the investigation section which describes the officer's actions.

Think of the synopsis as a bird's eye view of the incident, in its entirety

To read more samples of reconstructions for various crimes with lots of varieties of details, go to the samples section and read some of those.

The samples are where you will find a story of an incident, then, a reconstruction of that incident, then the investigation and all necessary interviews, details.

Segments of an Investigation

- Heading

- How you got there

- Who you talked to

- What you saw

- What you did

Writing the investigation

Now we get to the hard part. You have finished the fill in the blank portion. You have completed the reconstruction or synopsis, now it is time to explain what you did, saw, heard even smelled. In your own words.

The investigation will go on a big blank page, all by itself. There are no prompts on how to write it. There are no shortcuts, no drop down menus, nothing but you. You will write out what you did, in long hand. With great detail, not leaving anything out. Although this may sound difficult, when broken down it is really quite easy.

Ready?

What is an Investigation

The investigation is where you tell your story of what you did. You will go into your actions. There are only a few sections or segments that need to be covered in each report.

Let's go over each, in detail to see what they do.

The Heading

When you write out the investigation, open a new page in your word document or go to a new report page. Begin with writing out the heading of what you are getting ready to report. There are only 3 choices here:

Heading Choices

-Investigation

-Interview

-Details

Since we are learning about the investigation, let's start with that.

Police Report

Investigation:

That's it, next.

How did you get this call?

When you read the samples you will see lots of them starting out with calls being dispatched by a dispatcher. But, calls can be computer dispatched or even rolled up on, by you.

Why is this important to document? When you are on the stand, attorneys will ask you this. You may not remember months down the road. But, if you can remember, it makes you look very credible to a jury that you were able to recall such a minute detail.

List how you got the call. This puts you mentally at the beginning and gets things rolling.

Police Report

Investigation:

I received this call by computer dispatch.

This one is done.

Who you met with first

When you arrive, you will usually meet with someone. They could be the complainant, witness or such. List who you met with first. List them by their role, not by name. Role means, complainant, witness or victim.

Then stop. This is a one line explanation. This is also where things can go awry easily. Everyone, and I do mean everyone wants to write,,, *"and they said,,,"* nope, stop here. You will see why in a bit.

Start this next statement simply with:

On my arrival,,,

Police Report

Investigation:

I received this call by computer dispatch. On my arrival I met with and interviewed the victim.

Ok, how easy is this, really!

Emergency Procedures (this is a little sidenote)

On some scenes, you are going to need to jump into action before you can even get your car door open.

If someone is running from your scene, you may need to chase them. If someone is hurt you may need to aid them. If someone is about to hurt someone else, you may need to stop them.

This section will not apply to all reports, just the really fun ones.

Police Report

Investigation:

I received this call by computer dispatch. On my arrival I met with the victim, who was bleeding from a wound to the right side of his head. The victim was conscious and able to speak, no other injuries were observed.

I requested an ambulance, Fire Rescue unit #4 responded with paramedic Warren Piece, rendering aid to the victim.

Did you catch the paramedics name?

What you saw

Remember earlier, how I had you take in your environment when you were pulling up? Location, direction, people, just stuff in general. Here is where we get to write about that.

Some reports will have tons of details and descriptions, some reports are a bit thin on details. You create the picture, but in writing.

This is where you will get to go into detail describing the crime scene, buildings, rooms, skid marks, blood stains, injuries, all of it. Begin very simply with:

As I approached, I observed (heard, smelled)…

Police Report

<u>Investigation:</u>

I received this call by computer dispatch. On my arrival I met with and interviewed the victim.

As I approached the victim's home I observed it was a one-story, wood frame, single family home. The home was on the west side of the street and faced east toward N. 22nd st. There was a footprint on the outside of the home, on the siding. This footprint was under an unlocked window.

The front door of the home faced east and was glass etched, fiberglass door. This door had a double cylinder, dead bolt lock, which was intact.

This is your chance to get crazy with the details. Look through the samples to see what I mean.

What you did

This is the section where you write about you investigative skills. Here is where you list what you did in relation to, taking pictures, dusting for fingerprints, collecting evidence, returning property to the rightful owner and so on. Begin this with a simple:

At the scene I…

Police Report

Investigation:

I received this call by computer dispatch. On my arrival I met with and interviewed the victim.

As I approached the victim's home I observed it was a one-story, wood frame, single family home. The home was on the west side of the street and faced east toward N. 22nd st.

The front door of the home faced east and was glass etched, fiberglass door. This door had a double cylinder, dead bolt lock, which was intact. There was a footprint on the outside of the home, on the siding. This footprint was under an unlocked window.

At the scene, I dusted all affected areas for fingerprints. Several prints were recovered from the doorknob. These prints were sent to the lab for processing.

I photographed the footprint, both with a measure and without. Several more photographs were taken of the scene. They were downloaded and added to this report as an attachment.

Notice how each task is separated by a new paragraph? Separate the things you do, to make the report easier to read. The paragraphs will naturally flow together into a series of events.

You are categorizing your actions, and then writing them out. This is the most logical sequence and probably the order in which you actually handled the call anyway.

Here is what the investigation looks like when it's done:

Police Report

Investigation:

I received this call by computer dispatch. On my arrival I met with and interviewed the victim.

As I approached the victim's home I observed it was a one-story, wood frame, single family home. The home was on the west side of the street and faced east toward N. 22nd st. There was a footprint on the outside of the home, on the siding. This footprint was under an unlocked window.

The front door of the home faced east and was glass etched, fiberglass door. This door had a double cylinder, dead bolt lock, which was intact.

At the scene, I dusted all affected areas for fingerprints. Several prints were recovered from the doorknob. These prints were sent to the lab for processing.

I photographed the footprint, both with a measure and without. Several more photographs were taken of the scene. They were downloaded and added to this report as an attachment.

Writing the interview

By now you have read many times throughout this book, that certain things get written into the interview portion of the report. A few short samples are found here and there in this book, just to make a point. Finally, here are the real instructions for how to write out an interview.

Interview Basics to think about

- What is an interview

- Who gets interviewed

- Who goes first

What is an interview

Basically the interview is the complainant's story, being told by you. But, only after we fix the grammar, put it back into order, find suitable adjectives for their 4-letter vocabulary, and polish it into a legible, readable, useful statement. You got the information, for writing out the interview by asking lots of questions. Then, we summarize the answers in a nice, flowing, narrative style format.

This does not mean we put words in their mouth as to what happened. We did not lead their questioning or interview, we are simply smartening their statement up.

Who gets interviewed

Generally, a police report will always have an interview. You will have a person telling you how something happened. This something happened to them, making them a complainant. Or, this something happened to someone else, making them a witness. Or, they did this something to someone else, making them a defendant.

If someone is telling you something that happened, in any of the above classifications, and it important enough, they get an interview written out. Not everyone is important enough. If we need their testimony to for probable cause to arrest, they are important. If we need them to be a complainant so a report can be filed, they are important.

When you interview someone and they talked in circles, had to be put back on track and gave details out of order, this is where we fix all of that.

Interview Segments

- Heading

- Role

- Where were they

- What they knew

- What they saw

- Can they identify

- Do they wish to prosecute

Who goes first

Determine which one gets their interview written out first, usually it's the one that best fits keeping everything in chronological order. Again, list them by their role, not name.

Let's break it down

Each interview will have segments, just like the investigation did. When you write out the interview by segments, it becomes easy to see what needs to be documented in each section.

All the details get added in, in order, neatly. And, you get done quickly.

Let's look at these segments in a bit more detail each.

Heading

When you are ready to write out the interview, drop down a few spaces and make a new heading for the interview.

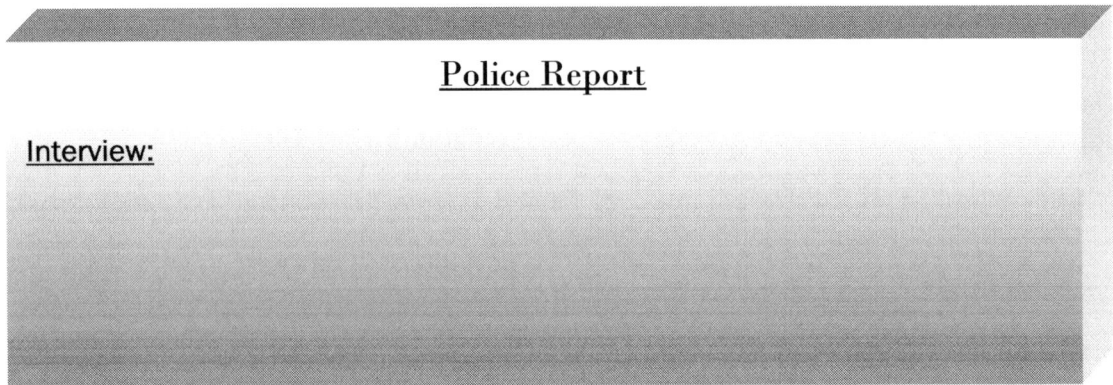

Police Report

Interview:

Roles

Roles describe who is being interviewed. Each interview is marked so we know who's story or point of view we are reading about. Do not list people by name, that gets confusing quick.

Stick to their role only so everyone knows how everyone else fits into the story.

There are only a few to choose from.

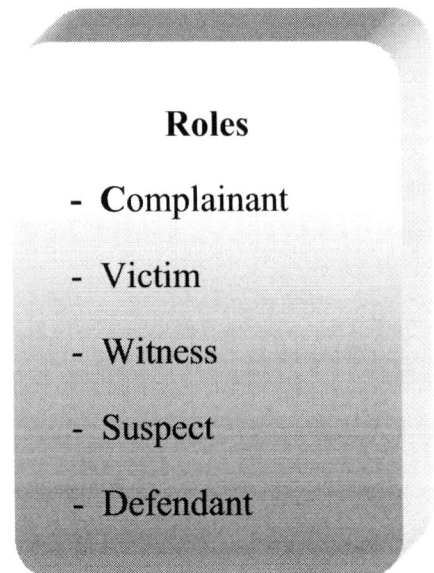

Roles

- Complainant

- Victim

- Witness

- Suspect

- Defendant

Role Sample

> ### Police Report
>
> <u>Interview:</u> Complainant,

Where were they when "it" happened

The next segment we list is where was the complainant when the offense happened. Most of the time this will be pretty easy, and obvious. But, to keep any jurisdictional issues covered, or to establish a time line in a delayed offense, document where they were. Start out this sentence with:

The complainant said...

> ### Police Report
>
> <u>Interview:</u> Complainant,
>
> The complainant said she went to bed last night at about midnight. When she got up this morning at about 7, her car was missing.

This put her at home, it also created a timeline for a delayed offense. Notice how we are not using her name? It is listed in the fill in the blank section of the report. The home address is listed in the fill in the blank section too. Date? Yep, look for that in the fill in the blanks too.

What they knew

Depending on your offense, this one can be all over the map. Remember to keep this part relevant to the crime. This is a great place to insert all those brilliant questions you asked during the interview, to pinpoint details of what may, or may not have happened.

Think of this format as a summary of the questions you asked. Not as a Q&A type of listing. Start another sentence, again with:

She said...

Police Report

Interview: Complainant,

The complainant said she went to bed last night at about midnight. When she got up this morning at about 7, her car was missing.

She said she is not late on any payments and no one else has keys to her car, the car was locked.

What they saw or heard (or didn't see or hear)

Again, your great investigatory skills got even more information out of a sleeping complainant, to pinpoint what may, or may not have happened here.

Sometimes people will hear things, but not really know what they heard until we interview them and tie it all together for them.

Very common with gunshots. People hear them, but assume they are something else. When we speak to them they do remember, and can sometimes even remember a time to help narrow down our investigation.

But, sometimes it can be just as important as what they don't hear. Drop down a line and begin this section with:

The complainant did,,, (or did not)

Police Report

Interview: Complainant,

The complainant said she went to bed last night at about midnight. When she got up this morning at about 7, her car was missing.

She said she is not late on any payments and no one else has keys to her car, the car was locked.

The complainant did not hear any sounds that she thought were unusual.

Can they identify

This is important for each person being interviewed. Can they identify the bad guy? It does not mean can they, write out a detailed description or work with a composite artist. It just means, can they recognize the bad guy if they see him again?

Most people will honestly say either yes or no to this without feeling pressured to perform, or be intimidated by law enforcement.

It is important to document their answer, whether it is a yes or no. That lets the daytime detectives and prosecuting attorney's know well in advance what they may be dealing with, with regard to this witness. Drop down a line and add in:

The complainant cannot,,,

Police Report

Interview: Complainant,

The complainant said she went to bed last night at about midnight. When she got up this morning at about 7, her car was missing.

She said she is not late on any payments and no one else has keys to her car, the car was locked.

The complainant did not hear any sounds that she thought were unusual.

The complainant cannot identify any suspects regarding this offense.

Do they wish to prosecute

Again, important for later. Do they wish to prosecute if someone is arrested? They may only need the report for their insurance company. They may have no desire to get involved in any court procedures, just write the report and move on.

Some agencies require them to at least want to prosecute for a report to be generated, some do not. Know your department's rules. Drop down a line and write in:

The complainant does (or does not) wish,,,

<u>Police Report</u>

<u>Interview:</u> Complainant,

The complainant said she went to bed last night at about midnight. When she got up this morning at about 7, her car was missing.

She said she is not late on any payments and no one else has keys to her car, the car was locked.

The complainant did not hear any sounds that she thought were unusual.

The complainant cannot identify any suspects regarding this offense.

The complainant does wish to prosecute if there are any arrests made regarding this offense

The finished interview

Just like the investigation, the interview is written out in segments. Separating each thought or subject by dropping down to create a new paragraph, makes the interview easy to read, follow and refer back to.

Here is what the complete interview looks like:

Police Report

Interview: Complainant,

The complainant said she went to bed last night at about midnight. When she got up this morning at about 7, her car was missing.

She said she is not late on any payments and no one else has keys to her car, the car was locked.

The complainant did not hear any sounds that she thought were unusual.

The complainant cannot identify any suspects regarding this offense.

The complainant does wish to prosecute if there are any arrests made regarding this offense

---

This is simple, this is basic and in a lot of delayed offenses where the complainant didn't see anything, this is very common.

Details

The last type of heading you can use is Details. Not the most common heading. But, it is the best to use when you are the on-scene officer, making an arrest. Or, you are the victim. Or, you are simply documenting something for a civil purpose such as found/ lost property, information for an insurance claim.

Police Report

Details:

While on foot patrol for burglary saturation, in the listed area I observed the defendant's sitting in a parked car. The car was parked next to an alleyway and was turned off.

Both occupants of the vehicle were seen passing a marijuana cigarette between them. Both were smoking from this same cigarette.

The vehicle had a very strong odor of marijuana coming from inside it.

Both defendant's were removed from the vehicle. The driver /owner of the vehicle gave police permission to search the vehicle for additional drugs or contraband, with negative results.

The marijuana cigarette tested positive with a chemical reagent test for marijuana.

The defendant's were arrested. Both qualified for Releasing on their own Recognizance.

These are the basic building blocks of writing out a police report for every offense known. You can add in lots of details to a crime scene where you did lots of clever investigative things. You can have longer interview sections where you had complex questions to ask.

Or, you will have virtually no investigative section if the offense was delayed and reported elsewhere.

If you can't wait to see more, go to the samples section at the end of this book. There you will find stories with all the accompanying police reports. This will give you a better understanding of what sections do apply, and how they apply so you can use them in your reports.

Chapter 4

Basic Grammar and other Dull Writing Lessons

This is the shortest chapter in this book. Why? I am not an English teacher. You are not taking an English class. You are writing police reports. I'm teaching you take blood, body parts, shell casings, skid marks and put them on paper. You will learn how to get all that stuff from the ground, onto an easy to write, easy to read legal document. But, with a few tiny, little rules in writing. Usually, legal documents are notorious for being lengthy, wordy with lots of commas and run on sentences.

Now, this is not a license to blab on incoherently with no regard to sentence structure or syntax. However, there are a few rules, if you will, that we should know about and follow because they do mean something legally. The grammar lessons that exist in all those other police report writing books are just semantics. Instructors being overly particular with no real working knowledge of how to document crime scenes or interviews related to police work. Great, if your purpose is writing perfect sentences.

If you are reading this book you have already taken a few college level English courses. You know what a sentence looks like. You know what a paragraph looks like. All police report writing is, is stacking those paragraphs in chronological order. Before you know it you have a completed narrative.

To get to that point of having a completed narrative, let's take a look at a few elements we will need, to begin stacking those paragraphs.

Stuff that makes up a sentence

Writing in the narrative portion of your report is easy. It is just a collection of sentences, stacked together to create paragraphs.

With that in mind let's look, quickly at the elements used to create the sentences to build that stack.

Things that make a sentence, a sentence

-Capitalization

-Nouns and Verbs

-Adjectives

Capitalization

Some legal documents are required to be completed in all capital letters, if handwritten. Police reports and additional forms are generally required to be in all capitals as well.

Some things that need to be capitalized without exception are the beginning of a sentence, titles, positions and names.

Names include people's names and street names.

Are you describing a car? Toyota Camry is correct, toyota camry is not.

Totoya Camry

not

toyota camry

If you have the benefit of using a word processing program, the spell check feature will generally alert you to the need for capitalization.

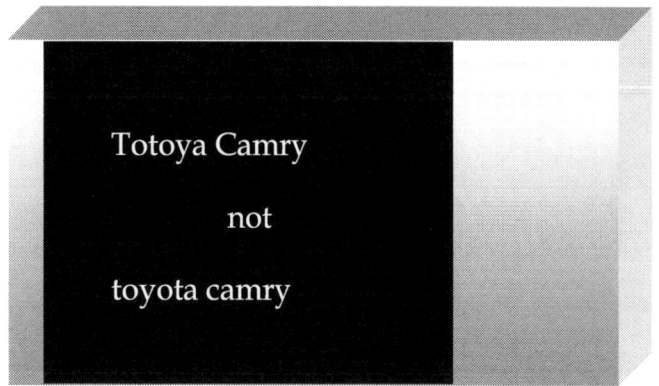

Nouns and Verbs

The two most basic parts that must be present for a sentence to be a sentence is a noun and a verb.

When we took English classes we had lessons where we underlined the action word, the verb twice. Remember, "if you can do it, it's a verb"?

Then we had to locate the noun. Underline the noun one time. It is the "person, place or thing" part of a sentence.

The reason why these are being described is they are the most important parts of a sentence. You need an action word doing something to, with, for, or at a noun. To have a smooth sounding sentence you must have these two elements present.

This is easier than it sounds. When we speak we usually convey information by telling another, something stupid someone else did. If the verb and noun are missing you will wait, listening for the rest of the story. The story is incomplete, sounds halted, unfinished. The same idea for writing a sentence.

Write like you speak. Tell the complete story line by line. Explain what the stupid thing was the stupid person did.

Noun Examples:

These sentences have the **_noun_**, also called the subject, highlighted**.**

> The **_prostitute_** offered the undercover officer sex in exchange for money.
>
> The **_suspect_** bled heavily from the knife wound in his arm.
>
> Upon arrival, **_we_** notified dispatch of our location.

Verb Examples:

These same sentences have the **_verb_**, also called the action word, highlighted.

> The prostitute **_offered_** the undercover officer sex in exchange for money.
>
> The suspect **_bled_** heavily from the knife wound in his arm.
>
> Upon arrival, we **_notified_** dispatch of our location.

Adjectives

Another part of a sentence to consider is the uses of adjectives. This is where you can have some fun. Adjectives are used to describe nouns and pronouns. Adjectives bring nouns alive, they also enhance action words.

Adjective Example:

This same sentence has the ***adjectives*** highlighted.

> The ***wailing, moaning, screaming*** suspect bled ***gooey, thick, bright red*** blood from the ***deep, jagged knife*** wound in his ***skinny, hairy*** arm.

Using Punctuation in your Sentence

Punctuation in a Sentence

- Comma

- Apostrophe

- Quotation Marks

- Parenthesis

- Ending

Commas,,,,,

When you write out detailed sentences in your interviews and investigations you will need to create a clear, concise picture of the incident. To avoid the words running together and becoming a mess of descriptions, you can insert commas to separate a thought, idea or wound's description.

Comma example:

The wailing, moaning, screaming suspect bled gooey, thick, bright, red blood from the deep, jagged knife wound in his skinny, hairy arm.

See how the commas clearly separate the condition, color and density of the blood?

Apostrophe'''''

Additional punctuation that can be used within a sentence is the apostrophe. For our purposes we will predominately use it to identify possession. Meaning who's what?

Apostrophe example:

> The suspect's arm bled gooey, thick, bright, red blood from the deep, jagged knife wound in his skinny, hairy arm.

Notice how an apostrophe is used to show whose arm is bleeding gooey blood? The suspect's arm, of course.

"Quotation Marks" How to say what they say

When you write a police report there is a very important form of punctuation that must be used correctly. The "quotation mark". This is a legal punctuation and must be used appropriately, correctly and perfectly.

You use these marks during the interview part of your report. Use these when you document exact quotes.

These quotes can be in the form of hearsay (more on this next) or, in writing down specific phrases from your victim or witnesses.

Quotation Example:

... "I was jacked!"

You could put this into the report. Then describe in the report, *(this is the common street term for robbery).*

Be prepared to clean up the report a bit so it does not appear as though the police officer is using and writing in that language. Not everything the complainant or victim says is important enough to use quotes. Save them for unusual terminology used by someone, or terms used by the bad guy.

Hate crimes will probably be your most important use of quotation marks.

Using these (parenthesis) things

When you are writing out something in either the investigation or interview, and you need to step aside to explain yourself, (use these).

Parenthesis Example:

... "I was jacked!" (this is the common street term for robbery).

Another use is describing a victim's account of how many bad guys there were. If you are trying to determine an amount and there may be more than one, don't limit yourself in your own words, on your own report.

The victim said the suspect(s) were running in all direction(s).

Sentence Endings

When you are done writing the synopsis, or interview or investigation, finish it. The right ending punctuation can close it up or enhance the meaning or purpose of the sentence that was just read.

Period….

When you are finished describing the gooey blood, end the sentence with an ordinary period._ Done_.

Exclamation Point!!!!

We will not use these very frequently. Only occasionally you may feel the need to use them inside a set of "quotation marks" as a quote from a victim, witness or someone else. They are the equivalent to shouting!!! Use them sparingly.

Question Mark????

Never, ever used one on a police report. Here is what they look like just in case you want to stir things up a bit????

Abbreviations

Taking into consideration the legal capitalization of certain words, you can also legally use abbreviations of certain commonly used words. It is standard legal format. You will probably have individual, departmental guidelines to follow, do follow those first.

If your department's guidelines are un-defined, here are a few examples of words that can be abbreviated and how to abbreviate them without legal ramifications.

People

-Compl.

-Vic.

-Wit.

-Def.

-Susp.

-Mr.

-Mrs.

-Dr.

-Ofc.

-Sgt.

Places

-St.

-Ave.

-Blvd.

-Hwy.

-Ln.

-Pl.

What Not to Do in your Sentence

Run on Sentences

When you have a though you want to get down in writing it is easy to write in a sentence that goes on and on which is exhausting for the reader and makes them forget what they were reading about in the first place. *Whew!*

Break this down into a natural pause. Say a line or a thought with one breath, then stop. Write that down.

Bad things in sentences

-Run on sentences

-Too many pronouns

-Too many names

Fixed run on sentence example:

When you have a though you want to get down in writing, it is easy to write in one long sentence. A sentence that goes on and on, is exhausting for the reader. This makes them forget what they were reading about in the first place.

However, legal documents, state statutes, and other descriptions of legalese, do not follow the rules of run on sentences, ever. They don't have to. They are the law and there is nothing you can do about it.

Keeping everyone straight in your sentence

Do not use Pronouns

When you write a police report you will very often be describing something stupid someone does. There is every likelihood there will be lots of stupid people involved in the same incident. You will have to describe them all.

Pronouns do this by taking the place of a noun by using I, you, he, she, it, we, you, they.

Everyone involved in your offense will have a name that goes in a special category on the report. Everyone involved will have a role: *complainant, victim, suspect, witness or defendant.*

The confusion sets in when you have to write the narrative, and keep all the people straight. It is not only confusing for you, but for people reading the report later. Don't overuse pronouns.

You were at the scene. You investigated the offense. You know everyone involved. When you write the report you may be tempted to write something like:

Example of an Overuse of Pronouns:

He hit *her* in the head. Then *he* smacked *her*. *She* hit *him* with a baseball bat and *he* ran off. *They* watched this and *she* ran after *him* while *he* took the bat from *her*.

This is a gross overuse of pronouns. But, I have seen this happen.

How many people were involved? You were there, this makes perfect sense to you. I am reading this in court a year later, I think there were 5 people involved. But I'm not sure. The overuse of pronouns makes this narrative impossible to follow. We'll fix this, keep reading.

Do Not List Participants by Name

When you write out the story of what happened in the narrative of the report, you do not want to list the participants by name. Here is why.

As you read the report, first you went through the fill in the blank portion. You probably skimmed this part. There were locations, times, charges, crimes and people's names. They were listed in a fill in the blank style format. You probably didn't memorize anyone's names, who does?

Example of an Overuse of Names:

Smith hit *Smythe* in the head. Then *Smith* smacked *Smythe*. *Smyth* hit *Smith* with a baseball bat and *Smith* ran off. *Smiley* and *Smithey* watched this as *Smythe* then ran after *Smith*. *Smithey* took the bat from *Smythe*.

Told you my examples may get ridiculous, but you get it, don't you?

So what do you do about this?

List all Participants by Role

When you write out the story of what happened, in the narrative of the report, talk about the people involved by listing everyone by their role in the incident.

You will know who the victim, complainant and defendant are. You will naturally know the victim was hit by the defendant. You may forget which role Smythe or Smith had. If you're confused just think about the reader. And, do you want to guess what will happen in court if you accidentally transpose the name of the witness with the victim?

Example of Role listings:

The *suspect* hit the *victim* in the head. Then the *suspect* smacked the *victim*. The *victim* hit the *suspect* with a baseball bat, and the *suspect* ran off. The *witnesses* watched this as the *victim* then ran after the *suspect*. *Witness #2* took the bat from the *victim*.

This sample leaves no question as to who did what. There were 4 people involved. And, as you noticed, there is more than one person with the same role, the witness.

The witness was then numbered. Why? The fill in the blank spot on your report form has the witnesses listed by name, and the spots are numbered. Follow that same position that they are listed while writing out your narrative.

Police Report

Witness 1.   Smiley

Witness 2.   Smithey

Putting it all together

Paragraphs

So far we have gone over the various parts that create a sentence. What to start a sentence with, capital letters. Proper punctuation within a sentence. Finally, how to finish the sentence with the appropriate ending.

When you begin to write out the narrative part of your police report you will write out a few sentences to describe a single thought, idea or crime scene.

Combine those sentences in a group of three, four or five and you have a paragraph. To make the paragraph flow more easily for the reader and keep your thoughts organized as you write, lead the last idea from one paragraph to set up the start for the next paragraph.

Example of a paragraph lead in:

The victim said he was drinking with the suspect's ex-girlfriend, when the suspect came into the bar. The suspect saw the victim and **walked into the pool table area.**

Once in the pool table area, the suspect took a pool stick down from the rack on the wall. The suspect looked back at the victim and started to **walk quickly toward the victim.**

As the suspect **came across the room**, the victim's ex-girlfriend got out of her seat. The victim's girlfriend ran out of the bar, several other people parted to let the suspect by.

Cutting the paragraph into sections or actions or ideas or thoughts allows the reader to stop and catch their breath. The reader can process the words and visualize the bar scene in their mind.

You can keep the description of the crime in order, and describe it in great detail. Naturally you will go from one act to the next and the next. Before you know it your narrative "story" will be complete, your report will be done, and you will be off to crush crime on another call.

Spelling and Computer Spell Check

Can you spell? Not many people can. In law enforcement there are a few commonly used, frequently miss-spelled words.

Fortunately today, we have at our disposal the ability to use word processing programs. Most agencies have a Word based type of program for you to type your reports on.

To access the spell check program, first complete your report in its entirety. Do not agonize over how to spell "misdemeanor" or "paraphernalia". Type it out phonetically. This means type the word letter by letter in the way in which you think it sounds. You will get that red, squiggly line under it. Congratulations you just miss-spelled a word. Leave it for later.

When your report is done, save it. Then use your built in spell check feature to make corrections. Save it again and send it in.

If your agency is still using hand written reports, spell checking a report will be done word by word, meaning write the correct spelling the first time.

Here is a very extensive web page of commonly misspelled words that relate to law enforcement.

http://www.csu.edu.

That is it for the grammar chapter. Not much more you need to know about this subject. I tried to be quick and efficient with no silly testing or practice exercises, I hate those too.

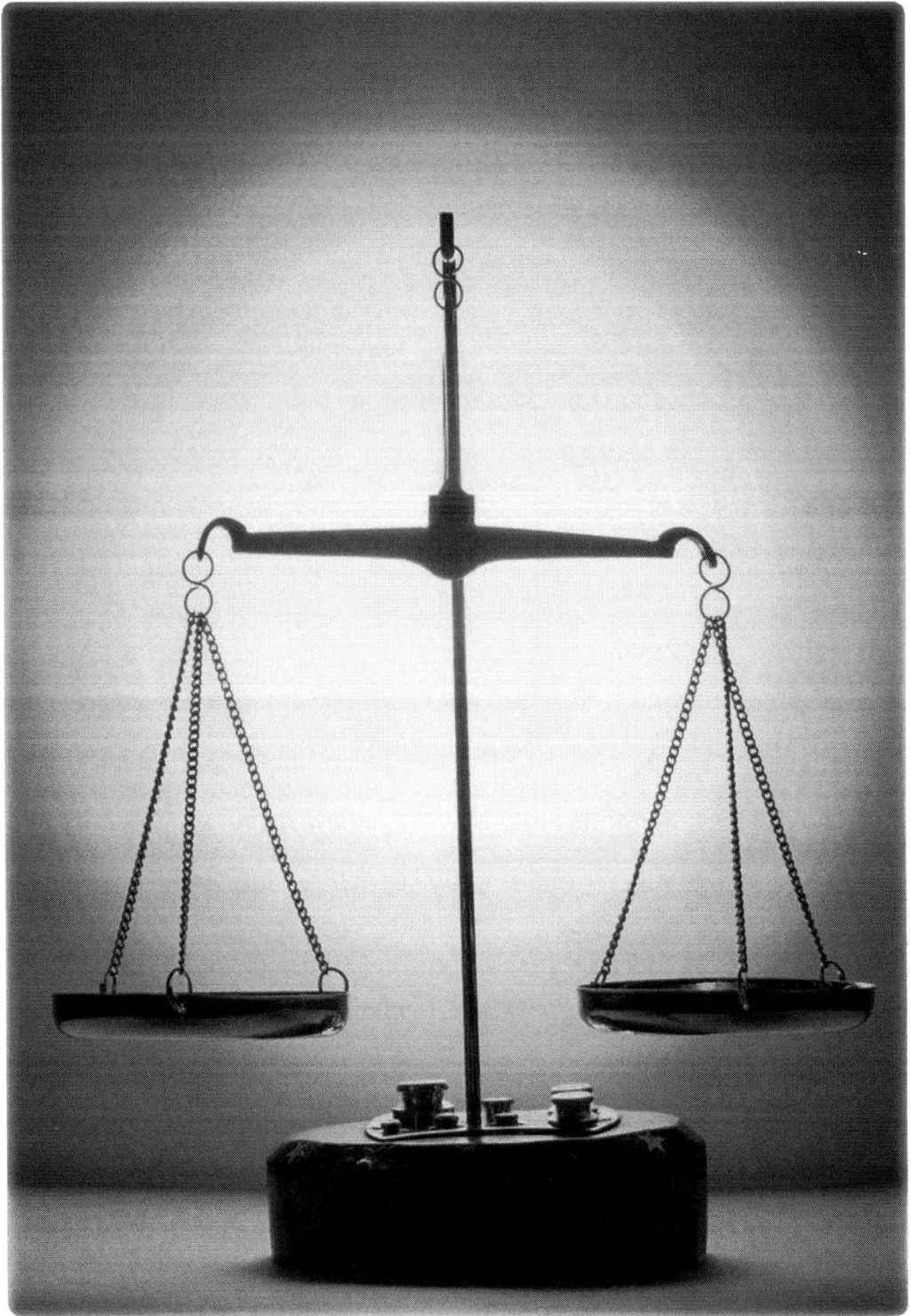

Chapter 5

Important Legal Stuff

" the law says"

The law says all the police report information, is public information. It is open to disclosure and must be available for inspection, publication and viewing of anyone who wants to read it.

Different states have somewhat different laws outlining this discovery. But, individual states also have laws that require certain types of "sensitive" information be restricted. These state laws are backed by various federal laws and are actually quite consistent throughout the country.

The legal penalties, for not only law enforcement, but entities that illegally publish information that is protected, are severe.

Privacy Issues

When you investigate offenses, sometimes they will be of a very serious, sensitive or private nature. I have had the question presented to me, how much is too much?

Are we really supposed to write those types of sexual battery details, or bloody crime scene descriptions in our reports? The answer is yes.

Sometimes your police reports will read like an "R" rated thriller or an "XXX" rated story. No detail is too private. No detail is too yucky, put it all in.

Restricted Information

Everything you investigate, or discover during your investigation must be put into the police report. But, not everything on the police report is public information. Meaning the entire report, even though you wrote it out completely, will not be given to the public in its entire form.

All states have laws protecting the sensitive information, victims, witnesses and even participants of certain crimes. Each state designates the originating law enforcement agency as the entity responsible for protecting confidential or sensitive information.

Redact

The term redact is as simple as knowing which information is restricted, and obscuring it. This can be done by marking out information on the master report.

Redact is the process of "obscuring or removing sensitive information prior to publication or distribution". (FJC, 2008)

The redacted, master report is then kept in a "restricted file". This redacted copy is the one copied and given to the public. The original, intact report is kept separate, available for complete copying for court and latent detectives needs.

What this means for the police officer writing the report is this: absolutely nothing. The victim's full information still gets listed on the front page of the report. All details of the victim's statement, "story" goes into the interview portion of the report. The details of your description of the crime scene and your actions at the crime scene go into the investigative portion of the report.

The report gets turned in as normal. The redact responsibility becomes the responsibility of the records custodian. They have to mark out the victim's information, prior to allowing the report to be distributed to the public, or news agencies.

Restricted from Public

-Sex Assault Victims

-Children

-Witnesses

-Juvenile Arrests

-Undercover Ops/ Officers

-Security Systems

-Shelters

Sex Assault Victims

Some people are reluctant to call the police, as a victim of a sexual battery. Victim's information is usually public information and will be given out. There are several noted, and really common sense exceptions to this.

All victim's, of any type of sexual assault are not

open to public information. This means adult victims and child victim's, their information is not given out to the public.

Not only is the personal information restricted, photos of the victim, victim's house and workplace and school information is also private.

However, this rule changes if the victim is murdered. The investigation becomes a murder investigation, that is public information, the details of any type of sexual assault are released and usually published.

Children

Child victims of abuse, of any type, are generally restricted information. Unless the child dies, again murder, then the child's information becomes public.

Witnesses

For obvious reasons, witnesses are restricted information. Ever try to subpoena a witness who lives in a car trunk, at the bottom of a lake?

If you are using a confidential informant for your investigation, list the informant by their number (C.I. #) as a witness on your report. The only way you would need to expose their identity would be in court. This is the time your prosecutor to tell the judge the open identification of the informant would jeopardize the safety of the informant, future cases blah, blah.

Usually you would be able to testify to what the informant told you during the investigation. This is not hearsay and should be admissible. If this does not work and the judge rules in favor of the informant being identified, this is when you can decide to dump the case to protect the informant.

Most judges are aware of how a confidential informant/ police relationship works and they will usually rule in favor of the confidential informant being protected.

Juvenile Arrests

The only arrests that are restricted, are the arrests of juvenile criminals. But, there is always a "but", their information becomes public if the juvenile has been, or is going to be adjudicated as an adult. This means the juvenile already has such a long or violent arrest record, the courts have already decided to emancipate the kid as an adult for all future crimes committed.

The youngest juvenile I ever ran into, that had already been adjudicated as an adult, was a 12 year old boy. I arrested him for grand theft auto. When we searched him he had three "hot wheels" toy cars in his pocket.

Arrests of adults are always public information. And, for some arrests that lead to convictions, not only is the information available, but it "will" be given to the public.

An example of this is the creation of "Megan's Law" which requires the public to be notified when a sexual predator moves into their neighborhood.

Undercover Operations/ Officers

Police officers get hurt. We get hit, shot, beat up, ran over, spit on and generally slapped around. If we are working in an undercover capacity, the bad guys may not even know we are cops, we can get knocked around pretty thoroughly.

If you are investigating an offense and the victim is a uniformed police officer, it is public information. In the address section, put the agencies address, not the officer's home address. If the officer is working undercover on the incident they were hurt on, then officer's name is restricted.

Your departmental press release can say an officer was injured, but the officer's name, photo and all personal information is very restricted information. This is a misdemeanor to expose the undercover officer in many states, and we will prosecute for identifying us.

By the way, if a police officer gets arrested, it is 6 o'clock news time. No restrictions here, you are done.

Security Systems

When you investigate a robbery or burglary you may come into contact with some pretty elaborate, expensive security systems. You will need to extract information from these systems for your investigation.

Usually it's surveillance footage from an older VCR or a high tech, digital, full color, motion activated system with face identifying software. Either way, the security system information is restricted information.

What you can say is the footage was provided by the complainant from their security system. Document this in the investigation portion of your report.

If the case goes to court the complainant, or security personnel will be the one to testify to the specifications on any security system. If the judge allows it

Shelters

Do you have a battered women's shelter in your area? Sometimes we will respond to these locations to take calls. Sometimes we will drop off our victims at these shelters. For obvious reasons these shelter locations are kept strictly confidential.

Radio dispatch does not even put these out over the air for fear of the average citizen listening in. If your call involves a shelter of this type, make sure you list it in your report as the shelter by name, but do not list the address. This is one of those bits of information that may slip by your records custodian.

If anyone important needs the address they can hunt it down or use the business P.O. Box, if they have one.

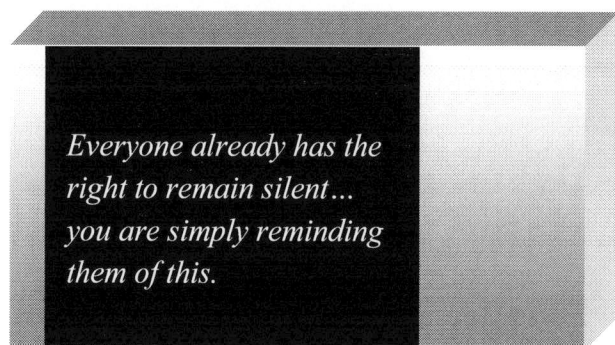

Everyone already has the right to remain silent... you are simply reminding them of this.

Overlooked but important legal issues

Miranda Reminder

Every person who steps onto U.S. soil has the right to remain silent. The person you are arresting does not have to be a citizen of the United Sates to exercise this right. When you ask a person a question, that you plan to use against them, and the person is detained or arrested by you, meaning not free to leave, you must remind them of their Miranda Rights.

You are not giving them the right to remain silent, they already had, and always have this right. You cannot give it or take it away. Remember this from cop school?

This reminder only applies to your bad guy if you intend to ask questions you may want to use against them. You do not have to read someone their rights if you are not going to talk to them. Not every person arrested needs their rights read to them.

Television loves to show this as the police forgot to read the bad guy his right, so the bad guy is released. Wrong! Silly movie legal stuff.

When you write out your police report, and you did remind the bad guy of his rights, document that in the interview portion of your report that you did so, and if he waived this right. Meaning he kept talking. It will come up in court later.

Alcohol

Special note: when dealing with an intoxicated person. Sometimes the question comes up, if a person is drunk doesn't that impair them. Can you

Too drunk to know or remember, is never a defense.

actually charge a person for a crime committed while drunk?

118

The answer is yes. Alcohol usually does help in escalating an argument to an actual fight. But, alcohol is not a defense.

Did the very drunk bad guy really mean to kill someone with a pool stick? He seemed to, at the time. Did he want to kill a couple of hours later when he was sober, maybe not? Will he still want to kill when he wakes up in jail tomorrow morning, maybe not?

If alcohol was a defense, every murderer would be drunk and not responsible for their actions and therefore not guilty. See where this is going?

The defendants level of intoxication must be noted and usually measured (blood alcohol content) but, not taken into consideration when charging your bad guy with a crime.

When you deliver your bad guy to jail, the jail will want to know just how drunk the guy is. Most jails will require the bad guy to have a BAC (blood alcohol content reading) prior to accepting him. When the BAC is completed, document the level or attach a copy of the reading from the BAC, if one is available. This will all be documented in the investigation portion of your report.

Hearsay

Hearsay is: what the victim heard the bad guy say,,,and told you.

Hearsay is defined as:

What the victim heard and told you.

You can put hearsay into a police report. You would include it in the interview of the person who heard it.

Example of Hearsay:

<u>Police Report</u>

<u>Interview:</u>   …the victim said the suspect told her, **"don't move, now go stand over there."**

When you write it into your report just make sure the exact words of the statement or comment are marked with "quotation marks".

As far as why this is important, bad guys will get into a habit of how they go about committing crimes. They develop favorite places to do bad things. They have favorite types of victims they like to prey on. And, they can even develop a habit of favorite lines they like to use when they do those bad things, including slang. This is also known as an M.O. (Modus Operandi)

Detectives look for such things when they review report to see if there is a tie in, in similar crimes. Your hearsay documentation might just link numerous crimes by a simple statement, statements that may get overlooked otherwise.

Also important, you the police officer will not be able to testify in court what the victim told you the bad guy said. But, the victim may be able to.

Help your victim out by putting the hearsay into the police report. The victim may be able to look at your report while they are testifying, or just prior to going into court.

The defense attorney will go out of their way to try to intimidate your probably inexperienced witness. They will make them look confused, stupid and dis-credit them in front of a jury. Keeping things consistent in court will go a long way toward a conviction.

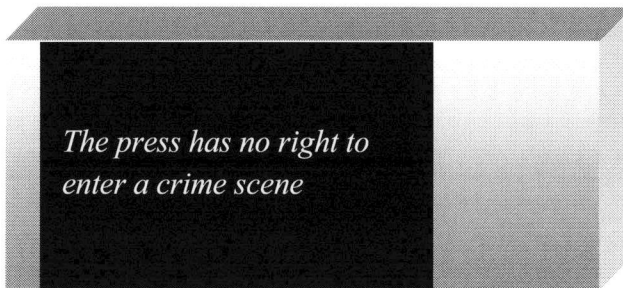

Dealing with the Press

The press has no right to enter a crime scene

When you are at a crime scene, the press has no special considerations, or rights to enter your crime scene. They will yell at you, try to intimidate you and outright lie and tell you the chief told them to go on in. Don't let them in until the full processing of the scene is complete. Then it is up to the property owner to let them in.

They are pushy, rude and will look right at you and try to trick you. Don't trust them. If they are outside your crime scene and they left their camera on a tripod, pointed at the scene, just know the microphone can be on. They will try to pick up details of your comments. The giant antennas on the tops of their news vans?

Those are sensitive microphones too. Watch what you say, you will find yourself on the news saying something that was only meant for your partner to hear.

Cops use gross humor as a way of stress relief. It is almost impossible to explain this to someone who does not have a high stress job such as ours.

Pictures and video at a crime scene

Digital cameras are nice. Easy to use, very convenient. Since many police reports are written in a Windows format word processing program, attaching pictures is a snap.

But, there are a few laws covering what you can take pictures of, at your crime scene, and what you cannot.

Photography in Police Work

-When you can photograph

-When you cannot photograph

-Don't move until photographed

-What the courts say

-Public domain photography

What you can photograph

Things that are allowed at a crime scene is, the crime scene itself. Again, when a location becomes a crime scene, it is ours. We get to photograph it, if it is of evidentiary, or potential evidentiary value.

> *Photograph all the blood, guts and shell casings you can find.*

An overview of the scene, the scenery, surrounding locations. Close ups of physical evidence. This does include blood, guts, fingerprints and body parts.

For a lesser crime scene, where you want to take a few shots of tire marks, footprints, handprints, bullet holes, take the shots prior to moving anything. When you photograph an item, place a measure next to it for size reference. There are small, plastic, yellow rulers that are made just for this. If you don't have one use money. A dollar bill is uniform in size. A coin works great for tiny items.

> *Don't photograph sex organs of a rape victim.*

Don't photograph these

Things you cannot photograph are certain body parts. If you have a rape victim and she wants to show you the injuries and begins to undress, this is not allowed. Sexual organs of any adult or child cannot be photographed, no matter the crime. Unless the victim is dead. Prior to the body being moved, it will be photographed in the scene, as it is.

When the body gets to the Medical Examiner's office it will be photographed thoroughly for injuries, marks, anything of potential evidentiary value. If you are at all in doubt, have your homicide crime scene team photograph your scene. Their equipment is usually better and they are very current on all laws.

Easy evidence destruction

If you move an object prior to a photo being taken, you can ruin its evidentiary value.

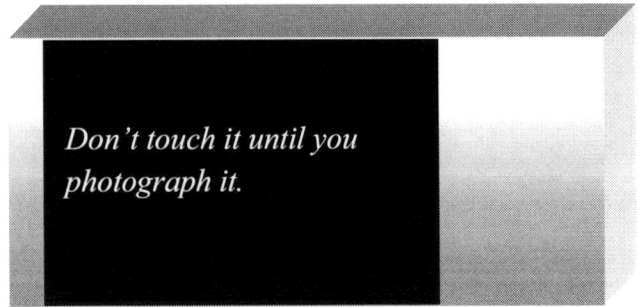

Don't touch it until you photograph it.

In fact, if your chief arrives first and picks up the gun to show everyone what he found, he just blew it. You cannot even photograph it properly now. You will just describe it in the narrative of your report. Don't forget to put in the report the chief moved it prior to your arrival. Chief's hate being subpoenaed to testify in court.

The same laws apply to using a video camera. Don't touch, walk around your crime scene with a video camera, audio on. It's a great way to detail physical evidence at a scene.

What the courts have said

Now, you may be wondering what the courts have said about using digital imaging technology? The argument has been, digital images are so easy to corrupt, fix, change or mess with they simply cannot be trusted in court.

Not so. In fact the evidence at any crime scene can be corrupted, moved or otherwise played with and changed. What this boils down to simply is, the credibility of the law enforcement officers.

The ability to use digital imaging in court are governed by the Federal Rules of Evidence Article X, rules 1001 to 1007 and are treated just like any other piece of evidence. Each state has a few of their own rules too.

Strong laws and strong support through case law allow law enforcement to use and benefit from this technology.

These rules state:

-Digital images are to be treated in the same way as other forms of visual evidence.

-Digital images are presumed to be accurate representations of what they purport to be.

-Any accurate representation is considered to be an original (ETM, 2004)

Public Domain Video and Pictures

If you are in a public place anyone can video record you. And, there is nothing you can do about it.

If you are in public, anyone can take your picture or video you.

Supreme courts everywhere have ruled your fourth amendment rights are not being violated.

Those same recordings are admissible in court, if you have done something stupid and get arrested. If you do some action in public, you have no expectation of privacy.

If a person would have a reasonable expectation of privacy, video surveillance would need a search warrant, if done by police. If done for security reasons (stores, private security) the surveillance techniques would need to be clearly marked.

None of this means anyone gets to put video surveillance into a bathroom or shower stall, ever, for any reason. (Humphreys, 2008)

Electronic Communication Privacy Act of 1986

This is a significant law that was considered a revision of the original law. The original law was basic and reflected the technology of its time.

The original wiretap law, now expanded to include everything electronic.

The original law, of the same name, made it illegal for law enforcement to wire tap into someone's phone calls. Police needed a search warrant to access a phone call. Police needed a search warrant, based on probable case prior to hooking up the wire tap and listening in.

In 1986, things were changing. Electronic means of transferring data were beginning to appear. Many more were being developed rapidly. And no, this did not involve Al Gore and his claim to have invented the internet.

Transmissions of data were being conducted between the military and universities, worldwide. Research was the main purpose. Pagers were becoming common place and cell phones were starting to appear.

These were not legislated as far as accessing their real time monitoring, or stored data. To protect citizens and provide a measure of privacy, the original law was expanded.

Its expanded version specifically includes, transmissions of electronic communication, data by computer.

Just what, exactly does electronic communication mean? Glad you asked, it means:

...transfer of signs, signals, writing, images, sounds, data, or intelligence of any nature transmitted by wire, radio, electromagnetic, photo electronic or photo optical system.

I don't think this leaves anything out, but I may be wrong.

This law is why we, as police officers need a subpoena, based on probable cause to access information that is transmitted or stored. We can get the information, as part of an investigation we just need to follow proper procedure to do so.

Email

Email is an example of protected electronic communication and storage requiring you first getting a subpoena to look at a bad guy's email account.

Even if their spouse says it is ok to look into their email and gives you the password to see what is in there, don't do it. It is not the spouse's email, it is not the mom's email either, get that subpoena first just in case there is something you need to use.

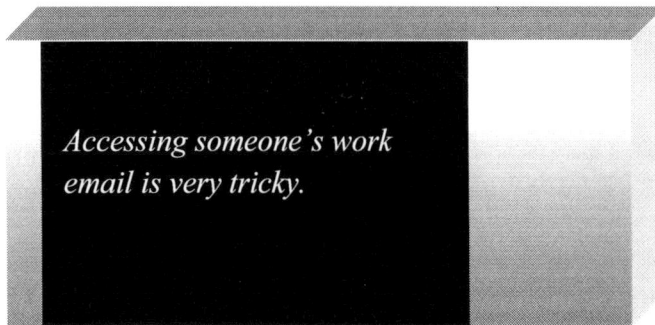

Accessing someone's work email is very tricky.

Work email

Work email is a bit tricky. If a law enforcement officer needs to look into an email, we still need a subpoena. But, if an employer looked into an employee's email or computer, found something illegal, they just might be able to look, legally. Here's why.

The employee does have an expectation of privacy while at work, working on a work computer. Unless a few things were in place first.

If the employee is working on their work computer and had to re-set their private password to gain access, they may have an expectation of privacy. If the access password was assigned by their IT section, then anything the employee does can be looked at by the employer.

If the employee is working on-line and the server access in through a private, employee owned server, the employee has no expectation to privacy. But, if the employee is on-line through a common server, Yahoo, AOL or any other server, non-private, the employee does have an expectation to privacy.

In addition, the employer has to have a written policy in place, signed by every employee stating the employer has access and will do random checks of email, hard drive content, email and internet, history searches. Then, the employer has to do, and document those random checks.

How this becomes important to us is, if an employer calls you to tell you their employee was downloading child pornography and had a few suspicious email's, they know this because they looked, a few things need to be done correctly so we do not blow this case in court.

Was the employee on a private network? Did the employee have to re-set their password? Docs the company have a written policy in place and this particular employee's signed copy available?

None of this means we will walk away from the case, it just means we will probably need to get a search warrant for the email account.

Computers

A person's computer is protected too. If we have probable cause to believe,,,get a search warrant. Anytime, every time you have to look into electronic, stored areas, get a search warrant. When you write about this on your police report, your probable cause, listing why you think a crime was committed and what the elements of the crime are, will be documented in the investigation section of your report.

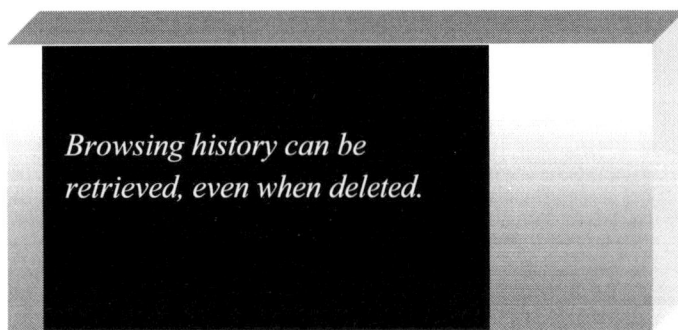

Browsing history can be retrieved, even when deleted.

You will list in great detail this probable cause and then reference the report to the search warrant. The search warrant will contain pages and pages of probable cause, evidence, where you intend to look for evidence, confidential informants investigation information,,,all of it. This will be signed by a judge and prosecutor, prior to being served.

Personal computers hard drives can be accessed. Internet searches, photos downloaded, even a web email account can be accessed.

Basically, everything that you look at or into, gets recorded somewhere in or on your computer, can be pulled back out and used against you in a variety of ways you don't even want to know about.

Trying to erase your movements through deleting cookies, files or histories is not effective and simply child's play to the truly geeky computer guys.

Chapter 6

You caught him, now what?

This is the paperwork chapter for arrests. When you arrest someone and they go easily, they are a yes person. When they simply do what you say, this is the chapter to show you how to write up that type of arrest.

If they refuse to do what they are asked, they become resistant in any way, the writing of the arrest paperwork is just about the same. But, there will be lots of information on what you did and why, documented in the police report? We will cover that in great detail in the next chapter, chapter 7.

This chapter will be mild, no killing or maiming at all, just the paperwork for an easy arrest.

Misdemeanor arrests, ROR or Jail

When you arrest your bad guy, there are two things you can do with them to complete the arrest process.

If the arrest is a misdemeanor and it fits your state's

Misdemeanor Arrest:

- Release (ROR)

- Jail

requirements for an immediate release, you can let them go home, without going to jail.

This is a process known as Release on their own Recognizance. If the misdemeanor crime fits all of the following criteria, and your agency and state allow, you can release them.

ROR Criteria

- The bad guy must have photo I.D. and ties to community.
- They cannot be wanted.
- They cannot have a history of failure to appear.
- They cannot be a flight risk.
- They cannot be a danger to anyone. (drunk driving, fighting in a bar)
- The crime cannot be the type they can repeat as soon as you leave. (trespass, battery on a spouse)
- They cannot have resisted you in any way. (fighting, running, lying about their name)

All you have to do is complete an arrest affidavit, or charging instrument appropriate for an ROR, for your agency. Assign them their first court date, their arraignment. They must sign this paperwork. Usually a thumbprint is required. They get their copy and they are released, to go home and never offend again.

They get to leave, without bonding out of jail. But, they are actually being arrested. The misdemeanor arrest does become part of their permanent record. They just don't physically have to deal with the inconvenience of being booked into the jail system.

Misdemeanor Jail arrest

If your bad guy has problems with any of the above criteria, he is not eligible to be released. He will be arrested, handcuffed and taken to booking. Once in booking, the jail may go ahead and ROR him themselves. Or, he may be required to bond out of jail.

Either way it is an arrest, on his permanent record.

The paperwork is pretty straightforward for each. And usually the paperwork is the same piece of paper or charging instrument for a jail delivery or an ROR arrest. This is because the charging instrument is created by your local prosecutor's office.

Your prosecutor needs certain things to be documented so they can look at the paperwork quickly and decide to file charges, set for a speedy trial, set a bail or release the bad guy.

This "all purpose" charging instrument is then handed out to all the agencies functioning within the prosecutor's judicial jurisdiction.

Speed, efficiency and consistency are the requirements and purpose of the charging instrument.

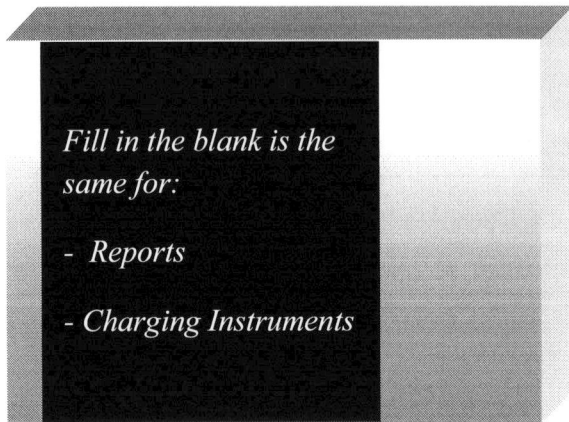

Fill in the blank is the same for:

- Reports

- Charging Instruments

Filling in the blanks of a charging instrument

When you look at the paperwork for the charging instrument, it will be predominately a fill in the blank style document. Complete it just like the fill in the blank sections we reviewed in detail in chapter 3.

Those lessons all relate to the fill in the blank for a charging instrument as well. The charging instrument will have spaces for names, addresses, evidence tied to the arrest, locations and dates.

But, an extra place in the arrest paperwork will be a space specifically for writing in the accompanying state statute or code you are charging the bad guy with.

This will usually be in a numerical code. Or, a combination of numbers with maybe a letter or two tossed in.

Statute: <u>810.02, B1.</u>

 The idea here is to point the reader to the specific chapter, section, paragraph and any subparagraphs of the crime you are charging the bad guy with.

Just a quick word of caution here. Most criminal chapters begin with a series of legal definitions for the use of a word in the chapter. These definitions are numbered too. Just make sure you are not charging someone with the definition of a crime, but rather the actual crime itself. Yes seems silly, but I get these tips from somewhere.

The Narrative

When the fill in the blank section is completed you will have a narrative section that needs a few sentences filled out, to explain what just happened.

> *The narrative is quick with two requirements*
>
> *-Probable Cause*
>
> *-Identification*

This narrative is supposed to be quick and easy, just like the synopsis or reconstruction we learned about, also in chapter 3.

The narrative is a blank space you will need to fill out. Just enough information, but not too much. There are usually two requirements or purposes of the narrative. Probable Cause and Identification.

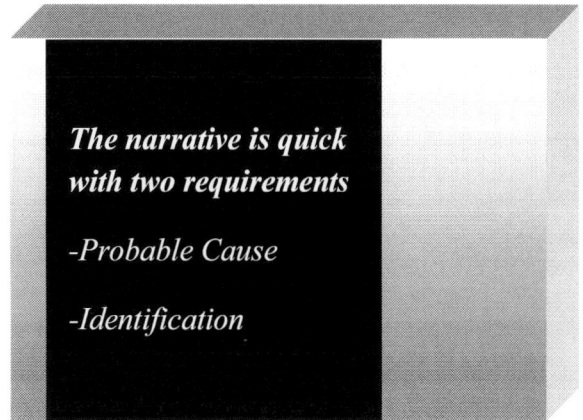

Probable Cause

The first part the narrative needs to have completed is what the probable cause was to prove there was a crime. Then, the narrative wants to know how you know this is the right bad guy that committed the crime.

This part of police reporting does not get written passively. There is no presumption of innocence until proven guilty. The wording should not even reflect this. The wording should be direct, specific and leave no doubt that the defendant committed this crime.

You should know the elements of the statute for the crime. Write out how the bad guys actions matched those elements in the statute. Thereby, committing the offense.

You do not want to repeat any information from the fill in the blank section. Just a quick, bird's eye view of the incident overall.

Again, easier done that described, so let's look at a couple of examples. We will use our story, from the sample chapter about possession of marijuana. On the charging instrument always start simply with:

The Defendant did...

This puts you in the frame of mind for just describing what one person did, specifically, exactly and precisely.

Charging Instrument

Probable Cause to prove crime:

The defendant did...

What did he do?

Charging Instrument

Probable Cause to prove crime:

The defendant did smoke marijuana in the presence of police.

That was dumb.

Identification Section

Is this the guy?

Ways to know you have the right bad guy

- Pointed out by witnesses
- Named by witnesses
- You watched the offense

What we need to know next is how do you know this is the guy who committed the crime. How do you know this is the right bad guy?

Did somebody point him out to you? Did somebody tell you his name and you found him? Did you witness this crime yourself and make an immediate arrest?

Continuing on with the same sample marijuana arrest,

Charging Instrument

Probable Cause to prove crime:

The defendant did smoke marijuana in the presence of police.

Identification of Defendant:

This offense was witnessed by the Affiant.

You cannot get much more busted than that!

Affiant is a fancy legal name for "who is writing this report".

It is you!

Who is he, really?

Next, the charging instrument will ask for identification the bad guy used, once caught. What this means is, how did the bad guy identify himself to you.

Choices may be verbal, or with a valid photo identification.

List whichever of these types of identification was used. State driver's license, state I.D., department of corrections identification. This does not mean a video store, or a handwritten check cashing card for identification.

How did you find out his name

- Verbal Identification

- Valid Photo I.D.

- Known to You

Charging Instrument

Probable Cause to prove crime:

The defendant did smoke marijuana in the presence of police.

Identification of Defendant:

This offense was witnessed by the Affiant. The defendant identified himself with a valid Indiana driver's license.

The entire narrative of an affidavit, when done and put together, should look something like this:

Charging Instrument

Probable Cause to prove crime:

The defendant did smoke marijuana in the presence of police.

Identification of Defendant:

This offense was witnessed by the Affiant. The defendant identified himself with a valid Indiana driver's license.

That is about it for the probable cause, narrative portion of the charging affidavit or instrument for a simple, on scene misdemeanor arrest.

Now, the details of how you snuck up on these people as they were in their car, and smoked marijuana, will be in your police report. The details of how the chemical reagent tested positive for marijuana, will be in the investigation section of your report.

To read this story and review this report to see how all those details get written out, go to the possession of marijuana report, in the samples section.

Felony arrests

The first way to arrest your bad guy is to ROR him, as we just went over.

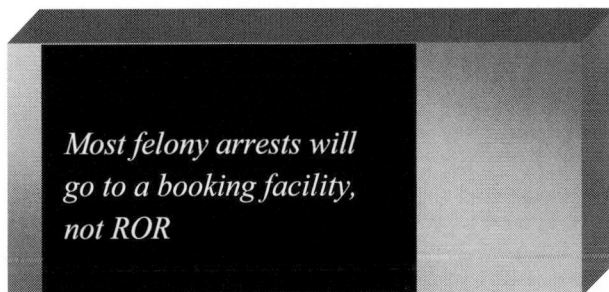

Most felony arrests will go to a booking facility, not ROR

The next way to process your bad guy is to make an actual physical arrest and deliver him to your local booking facility.

Your bad guy will almost always be delivered to booking, if they are being charged with a felony.

The writing up of the charging instrument or affidavit is pretty much the same for both processes. There is a similar fill in the blank section. Then there is a similar narrative section, where you will need to outline the probable cause and identification of the arrested person.

Many agencies have the same form that can be used for either a misdemeanor arrest of a felony arrest. Some agencies have a different form for each. You will know which one yours has, but the fill in the blank and probable cause still remains pretty similar and straightforward.

Next, let's go over a felony probable cause arrest. This narrative will be about the sample report titled Aggravated Assault, from the sample chapter.

In that story a bad guy was arrested, here is his charging instrument.

Just like we covered for a misdemeanor, the first part of the narrative on the affidavit:

Probable cause to prove a crime occurred:

Always start this simply with:

The defendant did

Charging Instrument

Probable Cause to prove crime:

The defendant did...

For an aggravated assault, there must be a legitimate attempt at hurting someone, very seriously.

If someone swung a roll of Christmas wrapping paper, there is not going to be any injury.

But, a pool stick will seriously harm or even kill a person if the impact is just right.

What did he do?

Charging Instrument

Probable Cause to prove crime:

The defendant did swing a pool stick at the victim's head, missing the victim.

The next part is, how do you know this is the right bad guy?

Charging Instrument

Probable Cause to prove crime:

The defendant did swing a pool stick at the victim's head, missing the victim.

Identification of Defendant:

The Defendant was identified by the victim and witnesses as the person who committed this crime.

And how did the bad guy identify himself to you?

Charging Instrument

Probable Cause to prove crime:

The defendant did swing a pool stick at the victim's head, missing the victim.

Identification of Defendant:

The Defendant was identified by the victim and witnesses as the person who committed this crime.

The defendant identified himself with a valid California driver's license.

The finished charging instrument should look something like this.

Charging Instrument

Probable Cause to prove crime:

The defendant did swing a pool stick at the victim's head, missing the victim.

Identification of Defendant:

The Defendant was identified by the victim and witnesses as the person who committed this crime.

The defendant identified himself with a valid California driver's license.

Some agencies call these probable cause reports. Some call these criminal report affidavits. Each agency or prosecutors office has come up with clever names for their own paperwork. But, the purpose of the paperwork is pretty much the same. It is the "get into jail" ticket for your bad guy.

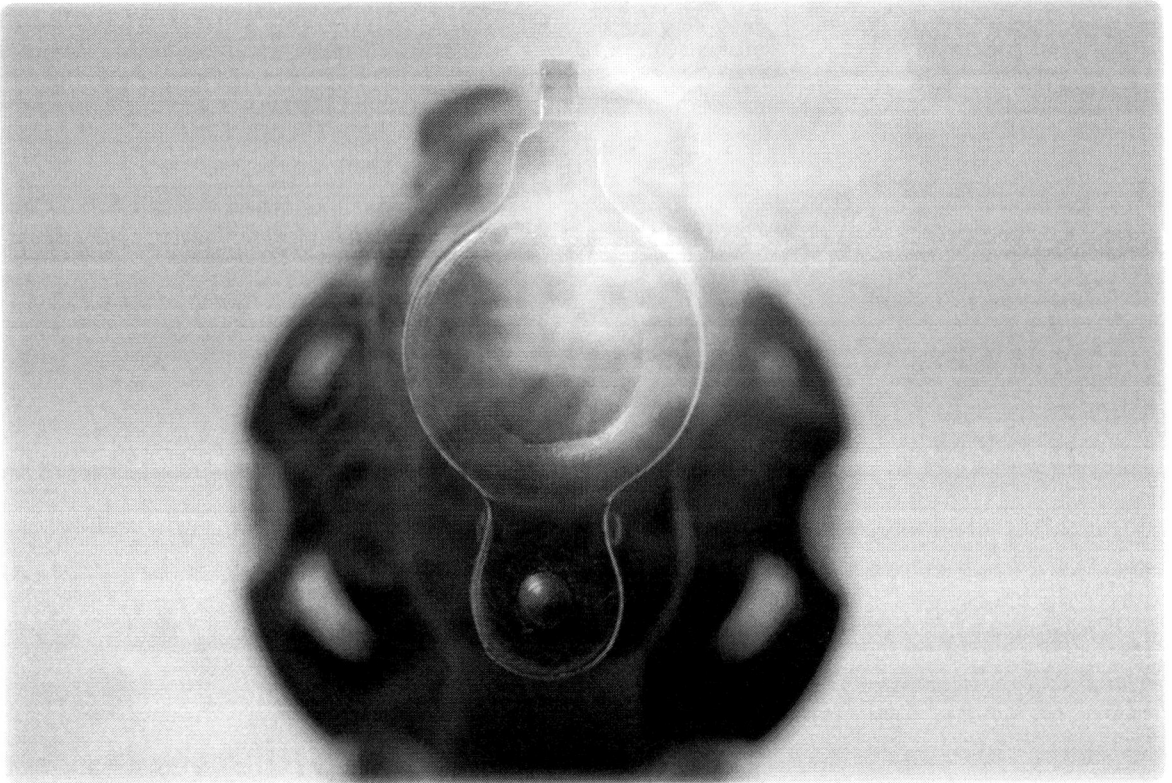

Chapter 7

Use of Force Report Writing

Police work is pretty easy. Once you get used to the long hours, smelly people and tons of paperwork. You might even think you get paid a lot for the seemingly simple work you actually have to do.

But, we do not get paid for what we do. We get paid for what we might have to do, that is when you realize you don't get paid nearly enough.

You will spend most of your time patrolling, answering calls for service and writing traffic tickets. Most of the people you encounter will be pleasant enough. Some may be a bit ticked at you, just because. Some will be greatly relieved to see you come into their homes. And still, some others will want to kill you on sight.

Most bad guys want to:

-Hurt you to run

-Hurt you to hurt you

These are the ones we train for. Most of the bad guys that you encounter will fight with you and do everything they can, just to get away from you. They do not want to go to jail and will resist just enough to be able to break free and run. Some don't. There are a very small minority of bad guys that want to hurt you just because you are a police officer, period.

Male, female, black or white it does not really matter to them. These people will usually have some history of mental issues. You may know this in advance, you may have no warning at all.

When to use force

When you encounter a suspect and you have to arrest them, the amount of force you must use to place handcuffs on a person is determined strictly by them.

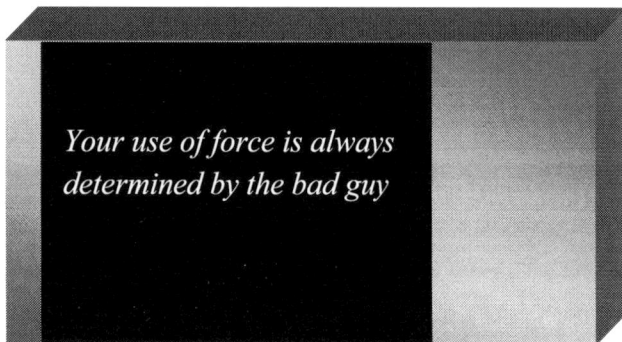

Your use of force is always determined by the bad guy

Every bad guy you encounter has the ability to place their hands behind their back, do everything the police officer says to do, and we are done.

Contrary to popular belief, police do not want to beat everybody up. We do not want to have to use even the tiniest bit of force to arrest anyone. Why? Tons of paperwork! We want everyone to stop doing whatever they are doing, put their hands behind their back and let us do our job. Most of the public does do just this. But, there are always the few exceptions.

Watch out for the cameras

The evening news has lots of live footage of the few who are the exceptions. Like you will read in the technology chapter, everyone has a camera. Most of those are video with sound too. In color, with zoom capabilities. This is where the conduct of a police officer is so very important.

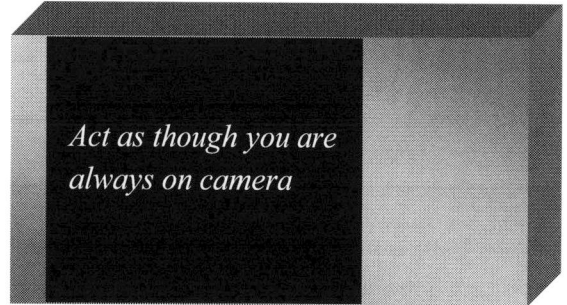

Act as though you are always on camera

On the news, there is usually a shot of the overweight police officer who gets there last, with the bad guy already on the ground. This police officer is usually the original one involved in the incident, it just took him a few minutes to catch up with the rest of the guys. And, this original officer is mad. As soon as he catches up and sees the bad guy is on the ground surrounded by a bunch more cops, this guy takes a quick kick into the bad guys ribs. Makes him feel much better. And the moment was, of course, caught on tape by an amateur photograper/bystander.

These filmed shots are grainy, dark, out of focus and it is hard to see faces. So the local news enhances them and just to be sure no one misses the quick kick in the ribs, the shot is centered in a nice, bright circle of light.

Why this is so bad

We cannot justify this kind of stupid stuff. This is an example of an out of control cop getting in a cheap shot. It was caught on tape and you are on your own. Unfortunately, this footage of stupidity taints the credibility of legitimate uses of force, also caught on tape.

> *News channels do not have to show everything that happens*

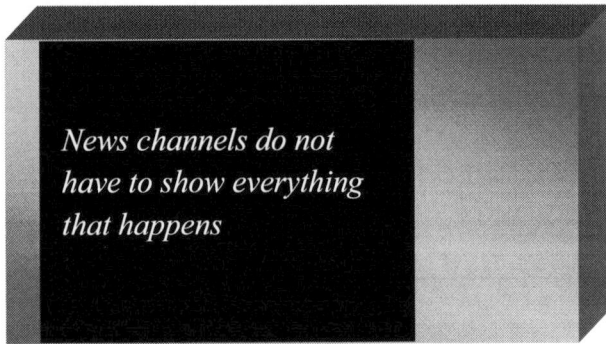

The shots showing a legitimate use of force, live footage make their way onto the evening news. The news channels are not under oath. They do not have to show the whole thing, just the good parts. And, the good parts can be the footage of 9 police officers wrestling the bad guy to the ground, while trying to wrench his hands behind his back to handcuff him.

It usually will involve several of the officers using various pain compliance techniques. The footage will show close ups of the weapons we are using. The footage will show the barbs and cables from the tasers, sticking out of the bad guys back.

Tricky news channels

What the heavily edited footage does not show is what happened just 15 seconds before. The really good stuff, where the female police officer was tossed over the hood of the car, by the bad guy. The part where the bad guy kicked another officer in the groin. Punched another officer and began swinging wildly so no single officer could get a hand on them.

The strength, size, volatility and just out of control wildness of the bad guy's action caused the remaining officers to escalate their use of force to gain control

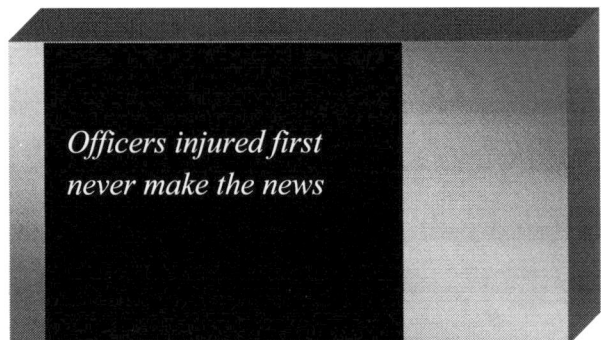

> *Officers injured first never make the news*

of him. They applied various pain compliance techniques then impact weapons and the use of the electronic control device to finally put this guy on the ground, so he could be handcuffed.

That is when the footage on the evening news starts. One bad guy against 7-8 police officers. The police are armed with various types of government issued weaponry and are using them all on the bad guy, who is of course on the bottom.

The female officer on the ground on the other side of the police car? A concussion and went to the hospital in an ambulance, no one will know about that. The officer he kicked, went in another ambulance and into immediate surgery. This bit of information will never make the news.

You, having acted with the appropriate use of force to stop the suspect and affect the arrest, for the safety of the offices and the safety of the suspect, will be under suspicion of police brutality. Because of corrupted news footage. Because of footage that will be taken intentionally out of context and shown over and over again.

You thought the bad guy was a good fight? Your next one will be against that news film.

So how do you fight this?

When you were the one following the rules? When you were the one playing fair? When you were being lawful? And, you still got your butt kicked on the street and then again on national television? How do you fight this?

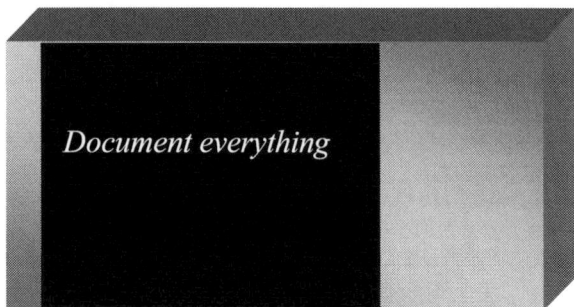

Document everything.

Always remember that in use of force situations we are reactive. Meaning, we will not use force if we don't have to. We tell the bad guy what to do and he does it, then we're done.

But, if the bad guy resists, then we will escalate to whatever level we need to, to control and arrest or stop the bad guy.

Resist by the bad guy can be on many levels. Our use of force to gain control can be on many levels.

Not all bad guys are built the same. Not all police officers are built the same.

The female officer that got thrown over the hood of a car would have to use a different technique or weapon to defend herself, effect his arrest and stop him, than a larger, stronger officer.

A male officer might not even get picked up, it may just be hand to hand from the start.

Now, the question may be, with all the neat police toys we carry on our gun belt, just how do we know which weapon to use first, or last, or never, or now,,,or when. Glad you asked.

Many police academies and criminal justice courses that teach any type of defensive tactics usually use a scale or model, if you will to teach you this. It is an actual visual reference to represent an officer, you individually

Your use of force may be different than the officer standing next to you.

and show you when it would be appropriate to use which type of force when.

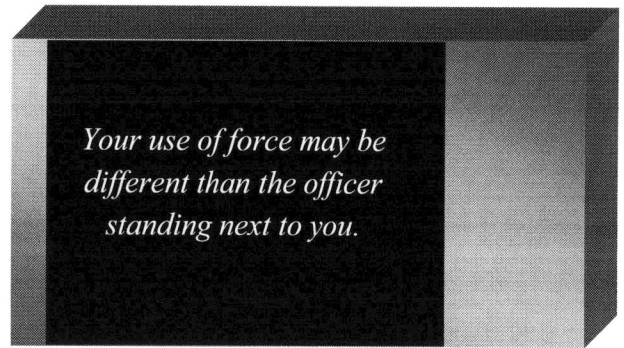

This scale is usually a very simple diagram that lists levels of use of force in official, approved, departmental terminology. Then, the scale shows what to do in response to a bad guy using that type of force against you.

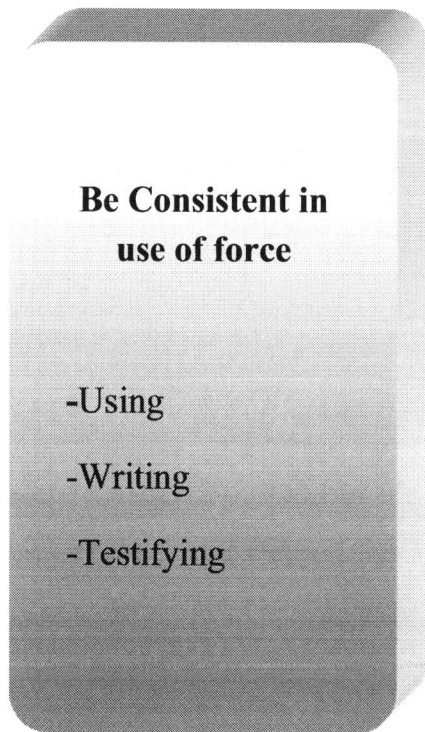

Be Consistent in use of force

-Using

-Writing

-Testifying

That is it, pretty simple. Visual, easy to understand and learn.

Its main use is to teach a police officer where they fall, in using force and what to escalate to and when, when using force.

But, its other purposes are to create a consistency within your department. Consistency in actually using force. Consistency in describing your use of force. Consistency in writing about your use of force and finally, consistency in testifying about your own use of force.

What to say, When

Since using force is such a high liability matter, you will be expected to understand why you use force, and then talk about it. And that is fine. You are expected to defend yourself and legally justified in doing so. When you do defend yourself and use force, don't be afraid to say so. Just say the right things, use the exact, correct, departmentally approved terminology, over and over when you talk about it.

When you do describe your use of force, that exact terminology, will include weapons used, body parts hit, how you connected with them.

When you take a defensive tactics course, you probably heard the instructor using terms such as "strike" or "deliver". These terms are used early on, in training to begin to condition the learner what certain weapons, movements and targets should be called.

If you are sitting in a courtroom, and you are on the stand describing what happened in a use of force situation, do not tell the jury you clobbered the bad guy. In fact, do not even tell the jury you "hit him in the leg with your nightstick".

Always sound in control

Hitting makes it sound like it was a fight. It sounds like it was a free for all, bar style, a bit brutal with damaging and mean police weapons.

Make every use of force situation sound intentional and controlled

It was not a fight. It was an attempt, on the part of the officer to control the suspect, to effect an arrest.

The defendant resisted and in an attempt to gain control of him you "delivered" a weapon strike to the upper portion of his left leg, with your ASP Baton.

You are such a nice police officer.

Terminology for applying force

Do use	Do not use
-Delivered	-Hit
-Placed	-Clobber
-Applied	-Beat
-Discharged	-Sprayed
	-Tazed

Terminology for body parts

Do use	Do not use
-Upper mass of the arm	-Leg
-Upper mass of the leg	-Arm
	-Head
	-Neck

Study your department's scale

Know your own department's scale or matrix or ladder or circle or whatever you have.

Know yourself. Meaning, know if you can use all your weapons and skills very proficiently, without exception.

Understand where your department places those individual weapons within your department's use of force scale.

Know

-Your scale

-Yourself

-Your weapons

For example, our newest and favorite weapon is the electronic control device. The taser. Some departments consider this weapon to fall within the pain compliance level of a use of force scale or model. Some other departments will consider the use of an electronic control device to fall within the level of an impact weapon. Still others will consider using the electronic control device to have its own category, just under deadly force, and insert its use there.

Each level's description is determined, department by department. Know your own department's use of force scale.

Variables to consider

In addition to the levels on the scale, there are a several variables that need to be taken into consideration.

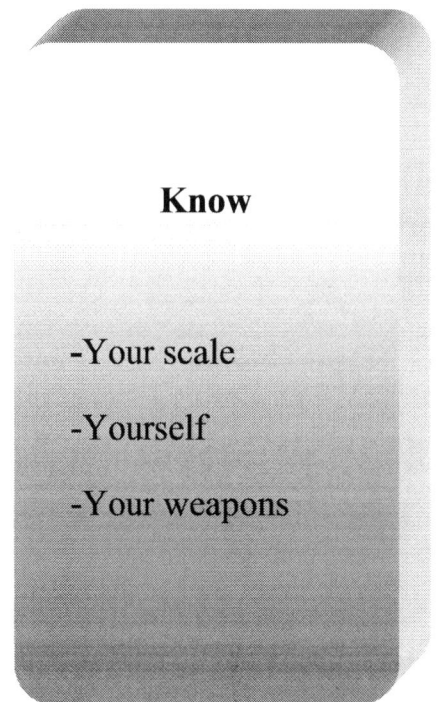

Other things to know

-Strength

-Size

-Skill level

-Environment

-Sex

Strength, size, skill level, environment. These variables apply to the police officer, and the bad guy as well.

Remember the female that was thrown over the hood of the car? When the huge, strong, bad guy put his hands on her, she could have gone right to a weapon, to defend herself.

Not much time to get one, pull it out of her gun belt and actually use it but, she would have been justified if she already had her baton, or pepper spray in her hand and used it on the bad guy.

Change this to,,, the throw would have put her right into an open traffic lane. She could have justifiably escalated right to deadly force.

However, a big, heavy, strong male police officer, would not even get picked up. He may only need to use a pain compliance technique to gain control of the suspect to affect an arrest.

Variables apply to the police and the bad guy

The difference in using a weapon or using pain compliance is determined by the police officer vs. the bad guy's size, skill, strength, environment and yes sex. Girls are not as strong as guys. Everybody knows this. Including the bad guy.

Girl police officers are different than boy police officers

Don't get offended here, use that fact to your advantage. Be prepared to document and testify to your known weaknesses. Understand why you may need to escalate your use of force differently than the big police officer next to you.

Remember in defensive tactics classes where you learned hands on, pain compliance techniques on your classmates? You could not even turn the guy's wrists to get them into a hold, unless they let you. But, the

> *Be prepared to testify to your known weaknesses*

guys had no trouble twisting you right into any position they wanted. What you learned in those classes were a couple of things.

First you learned what you could do, but most importantly what you could not. Do not go out on the street thinking you can just grab any old bad guy, put him into a pain compliance technique, and he automatically gives up due to your superior skill.

Not going to happen. If you could not put your classmate into those holds, apply a proper pain compliance technique to gain control of your suspect/ classmate in a very controlled situation, the classroom. There is no way you're going to ever get a bad guy, that does not want to go with you, go by you simply twisting him into a nice pretty pain compliance technique. Even with speed and surprise thrown in.

You will get hurt. You might even get thrown over the hood of a car.

Understand your own physical limitations, and understand how to fit yourself into a level of the use of force diagram or model.

Now, on the other hand, if you're a big guy that weighs 280 and you spent the last 9 years laying brick or working as a courier of cement bags, your physical situation would be different.

If the bad guy came at you and tried to pick you up, and you simply put your hand in the center of his forehead while you spun him around and neatly handcuffed him, your need to go to a weapon would not be there.

Two identical situations of a bad guy coming at you, but two very different reactions by two very different police officers to get the same result.

Use of force model

We have reviewed why cops get hurt, when to use force, what to say when you use force, how to justify your use of force. We covered knowing your department's scale, variables that influence that scale, so finally let's take a look at one of those scales.

This scale shows just the bad guys actions in clockwise, escalating order.

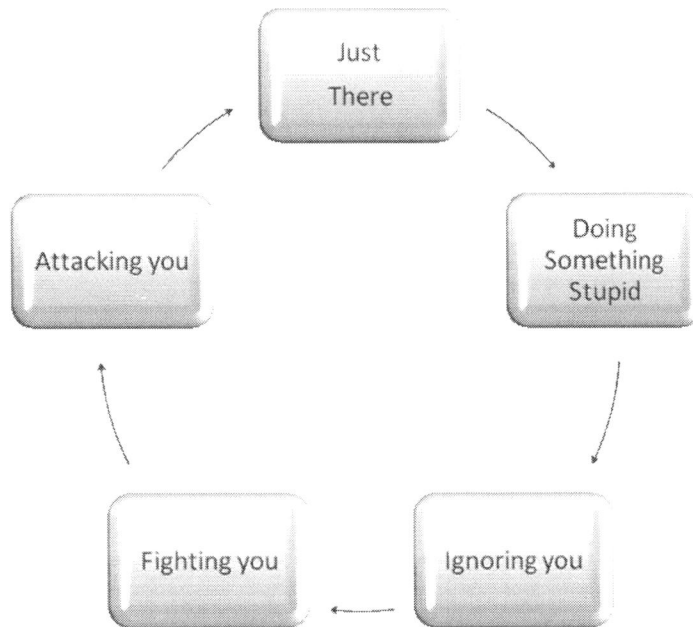

Just There

Doing Something Stupid

Attacking you

Ignoring you

Fighting you

Bad guy's actions

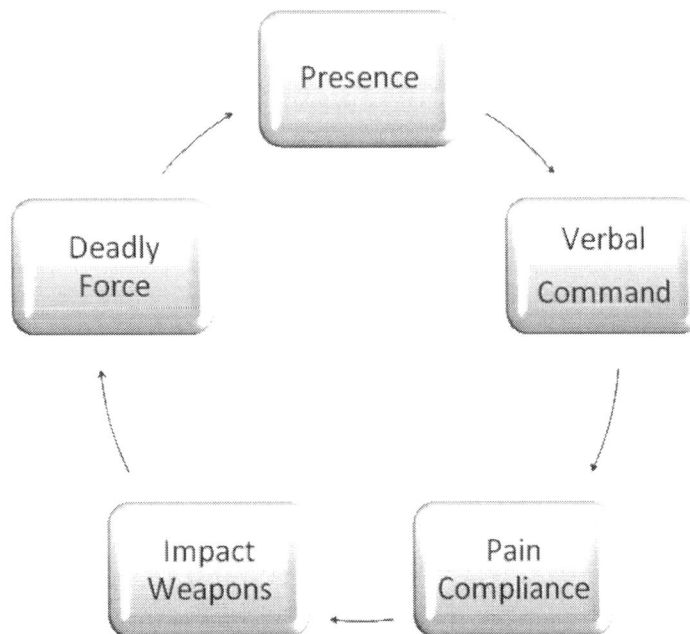

Presence

Verbal Command

Deadly Force

Pain Compliance

Impact Weapons

Police Officer's Reactions

Stack them on top of each other. The bad guys actions cause the police officer to react. For example. The bad guy is doing something stupid, we give them a verbal command to stop. Match up the bad guys actions and police officer's reactions, all the way around the circle.

This scale is what is known as a use of force model. You may know something like this as a Confrontational Continuum ™, force continuum, use of force model,,, lots of clever names that all try to describe the same diagram.

Starting with the beginning of the model, and demonstrating the least possible use of force, let's go over how we read and use the model to justify our use of force.

Presence

A police officers use of force usually begins at the top of the scale with "presence". We show up dressed like cops and bad guys stop doing bad things. The only mention of this on your police report should be, "I arrived".

Police Report

Investigation: I received this call via voice dispatch. On my arrival the crowd dispersed and I met with the compl.

You didn't even have to speak to or touch anyone. You didn't technically use force in a physical way, but we have to start somewhere so the level of "presence" was created.

Verbal Command

Moving clockwise to the next level, once you arrive and people do not stop doing what they are doing you may have to order them, or yell at them, to knock it off. This does include identifying yourself, just in case they missed the uniform.

Your report should include the fact that you had to identify yourself, or issue a verbal command to get compliance. On your report, you should put into quotes exactly what that very professional verbal command was that you said.

Put the command in quotes for a couple of reasons. Later, testifying in court the attorney will ask you what you said. Refreshing from your police report you will know exactly what you said, to the bad guy. Your internal affairs complaint will have your exact statement, because you refreshed from your report there too.

Put your statements in "quotations"

Refresh from your own report whenever you testify

This is creating a consistency in your verbal conduct. You put what you said in a report. You testified exactly in internal affairs when the complaint came in. You testified in court as to the exact same statement in the courtroom.

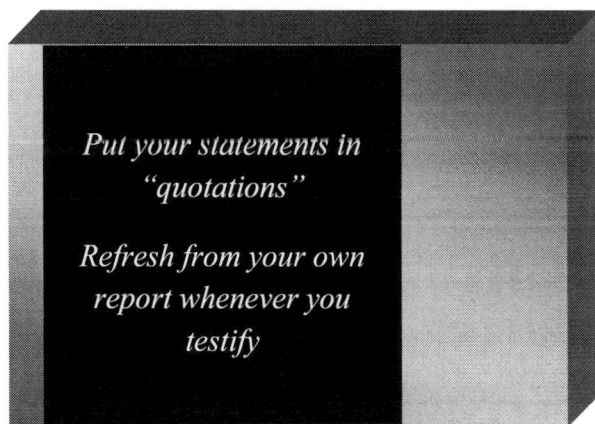

That complaint that you were a foul-mouthed, racist cop screaming obscenities, just got trashed. You wrote your statement down and testified in two places as to the exact terminology of what you said. The bad guy does not have these things written down and I'll just bet he isn't as consistent, or have as good of a memory. Guess who just won this one?

Just like the first level of "presence", you are not touching anyone or using physical force, per se. But, the bad guy does have to comply or you will escalate your use of force to gain compliance and control.

Document your statements in your investigative section of your report. Again, put your statement in quotations, and if significant, put their response in quotations as well.

Police Report

Investigation: I received this call via voice dispatch. On my arrival the suspect was in the center of crowd swinging his fists at several people.

I approached the suspect in the center of the crowd and ordered him to "stop fighting".

Passive Resist

Moving around to the next level, your model may have something called resist. There are usually two different types of resist, passive and active/aggressive.

Passive can be the protesters that just sit and ignore your presence. They ignore your verbal commands to move out of the road, private property or sidewalk. Their plan is to sit and just be a lump, in the way. This forces police to physically remove them from whatever area they are trespassing on.

Or, you might have a bad guy who just stands there and refuses to put his hands behind his back. Or still, the one that rolls onto his hands, on the ground and three of you cannot even pry them out to handcuff them behind his back.

These people are not fighting back they are just freezing up on you, refusing to cooperate.

If you gave the bad guy a verbal command and they refuse, be prepared to follow it up and finish with your job. You are not expected to fight fair. Meaning, if they are resisting passively, you are not expected to only use hand to hand, pulling and tugging. You will get exhausted quickly, you will be ineffective and you will look stupid and useless to all the bystanders.

This is why we learned all those great pain compliance techniques. Joint manipulation, pressure points, and the use of small batons to enhance the experience.

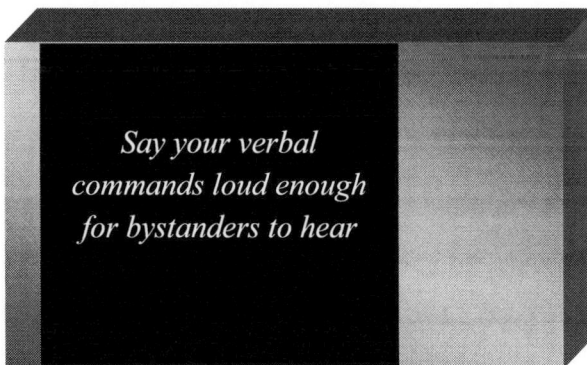

Say your verbal commands loud enough for bystanders to hear

These are very subtle uses of force by you, determined by the bad guy. When you use this type of force it should always be accompanied by verbal commands from you. Very simple, consistent ones so everyone can hear and understand what you want.

When you state your verbal commands simply, loudly and consistently, everyone can see what the bad guy is **not** doing , and his resistance. It becomes obvious to him and all the bystanders, including the news cameras. You are fully justified in your use of force, and everyone there saw it, and understood it as well.

When you write your report, this use of force will be documented under the investigative section.

Talk the reader through what was happening on your arrival, your verbal commands that were ignored. Then, list the pain compliance techniques you

> *List pain compliance techniques you use by your departments exact terminology*

used. List these by your department's exact terminology and spelling. List how many times the suspect forced you to use your pain compliance techniques. List how they were applied and where, with what result. Step by step, list your escalation necessary to gain compliance.

Then document what technique finally worked. Document the fact you stopped immediately upon his compliance,
and he was handcuffed.

And, don't forget the most important part. You immediately checked the suspect for injuries, from your use of pain compliance techniques or any other previous injuries.

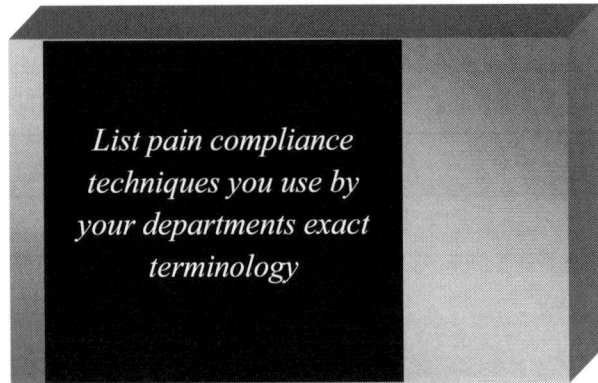

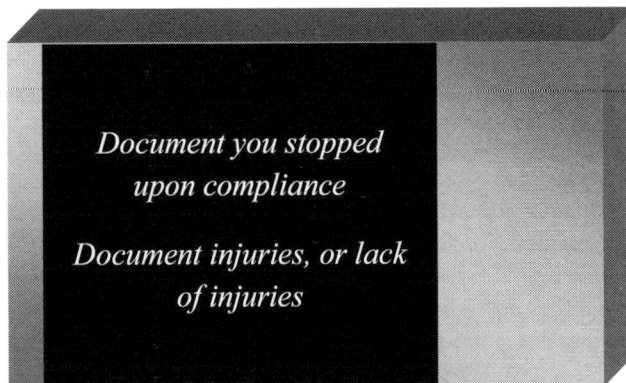

> *Document you stopped upon compliance*
>
> *Document injuries, or lack of injuries*

If there is a red mark on his wrist, document that. He refused medical attention, document that too. Then, when his injury complaint comes in six months later that he suffered a broken hand, by you, the complaint simply will not hold water.

Document this use of force to look something like this:

Police Report

Investigation: I received this call via voice dispatch. On my arrival the crowd was fighting. I approached the suspect in the center of the crowd and ordered him to "stop fighting".

The suspect immediately stopped. I told the suspect he was under arrest and to put his hands behind his back. The suspect immediately sat down, on his hands and refused to move.

I approached the suspect from behind and again ordered him to "put your hands behind your back".

The suspect did not move or respond to my verbal commands. At that time I applied an (insert departmentally approved joint-manipulation technique here) to his (approved and certified body part).

The defendant immediately complied with my repeated request to "put your hands behind your back".

I placed handcuffs on the suspect without further incident. I immediately checked the suspect for injuries. I observed no injuries or markings on him. He complained of no injuries.

Resist Active or Aggressive

Stepping it up just a bit, again because the bad guy has forced you to, we move to the next level of resist. Active or aggressive resist.

This is the area where different departments can agree to disagree on which impact weapons fall in this category. This is also where your reaction to the bad guy's active resist can be different too. Know your department's expectations with active resist.

Active or aggressive resistance is just that resist, but not attack. The bad guy is trying really hard to get away from you, but not to the point where they are turning and attacking you, or trying to hurt you.

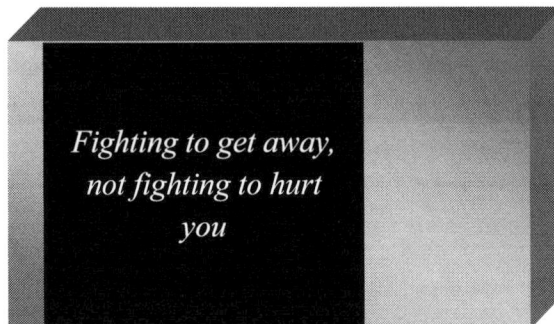

Fighting to get away, not fighting to hurt you

You are fighting with the bad guy. He knows he is under arrest because you told him, verbally. He may not have refused verbally, but his actions say no. He refuses to put his hands behind his back. He is rolling around on the ground refusing to show his hands. He ran, causing you to chase him.

Your pain compliance techniques did not work, you tried or, his resistance has not allowed you to even attempt to apply your pain compliance techniques on him. He is kicking out at you, pushing you away, and trying everything he can to get out from under you, around you so he can run off.

Actively resisting. Not attacking.

You can enter the use of force scale at any level, determined by the bad guy

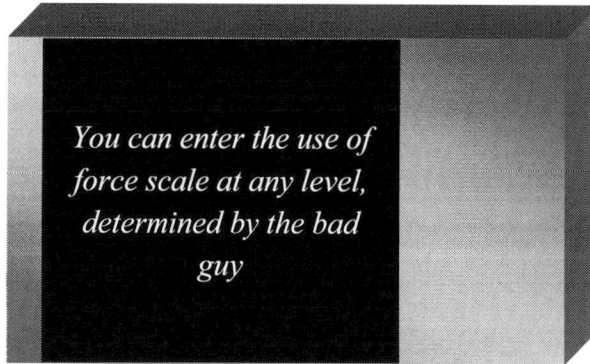

If you manage to get a hold of him and he refuses to put his hands behind his back, you will have to force him to comply. You do not fight fair, we always keep the upper hand when it comes to applying techniques and weaponry. If he brings a fist to a fight, we bring a police baton, type of thinking.

Depending on the amount of officers involved, the proximity of police falling all over into the pile, this factor should be used to determine which weapon you may want to use. With bunches of police around, you may not want to expand you're A.S.P. baton and deliver a strike.

But pepper spray? All you have to do is pull out your can, shake it and yell "spray"! The cops don't even have to move, just turn their heads and hold their breath. The bad guy gets a nice blast in the center triangle of his facial area. This causes a non-voluntary reaction called bletharospasm. That is a fancy, technical term for eyes slamming shut, coughing, spitting and snotting all over everyone. He gets handcuffed and hopefully the fight is over.

Check him for breathing, move him to an open area so the oils in the spray can dry. Not in your police car! Stay with him until the residue dries then load him in the car.

He will be in pain, he will be yelling, or this just may take the wind right out of his sails. Check him for injuries, so you can document this in your police report.

Write up your actions in the investigation section to look something like this:

Police Report

Investigation: I received this call via voice dispatch. On my arrival the suspect was in the center of the crowd, swinging his fists at several people.

I approached the suspect in the center of the crowd and ordered him to "stop fighting".

The suspect continued to swing his fists at other people around him. I approached the suspect from behind and again ordered him to "put your hands behind your back".

The suspect looked at me, stopped and began to put his hands behind his back. As I placed his right wrist into a handcuff, he **began to run**.

I held onto the handcuff and we both immediately fell to the ground. Once on the ground the suspect tried to **roll away** from me and get back to his feet. The suspect was **twisting his handcuffed arm, trying to break free** of my hold.

At this time Ofc. Smith approached and removed her pepper spray from her gun belt. She moved to the suspect's head and told the suspect "do not move". The suspect saw the pepper spray can in her hand, pointed at his face and **began kicking out** at both of us.

Police Report

<u>Investigation Continued:</u>

Ofc. Smith delivered a two second, single spray of Oleoresin Capsicum to the suspect's lower face. (see Ofc. Smith's supplement)

The suspect coughed, stopped moving and allowed me to place his left hand into the remaining handcuff.

The suspect was placed on his side and allowed to remain there until the residue from the Oleoresin Capsicum oils dried. The suspect was checked for injuries. The suspect had redness on his face in the pattern of the oils. He was breathing freely. No other injuries were observed. He complained of no injuries.

Once dry, the defendant was placed into my police car and delivered to booking.

Assault, Attack

The next level is assault. This is when the bad guy aggressively, physically attacks you. He comes after you, not away from you and wants to hurt you.

This is where I would consider myself falling, in the throwing over the hood of the car incident. If someone were to even come at me, I

We always escalate to get, keep or re-establish control

would go on high alert. If they got their hands on me, even worse. If my feet started to go off the ground, I would be kicking and swinging my baton like crazy trying to connect with something bony and exposed.

If your bad guy squares off on you and drops into a boxer stance, you are not going to box him. He just brought a set of fists to an impact weapon fight.

Most all of your impact weapons will fall cleanly and clearly here for your return defense and use of force.

Impact weapons can be many things. They are considered "less lethal use of force". These weapons can be the obvious ones, your police baton, chemical sprays, electronic control devices, using a police K-9, rubber bullets even PITT, with your police vehicle. But, it can also include the less obvious ones too. Your ticket book, clipboard, flashlight, and police radio.

Non-common weapons

We used to teach a class on using a ticket book on a bad guy, in a defensive manner. If attacked, and the ticket book was what you just happened to be holding, we used it. A couple of bad guys got some very nice cuts from the metal edges of these ticket books. They started it.

If you have it in your hand and you use it for defense, it will usually be a reactionary response. Probably a split-second reaction, hands up while stepping back, type of purely defensive measure. And that is fine. If you use a non-common item as a weapon, don't freak out and try to think of ways to re-create what just happened. Tell the truth. Think through why you did what you did, you will probably be completely justified.

However,,,

Something to remember, when you use an approved weapon in an approved manner, properly trained and certified by your agency, and you properly justify your actions, you can still get sued. If this happens, the manufacturer of the

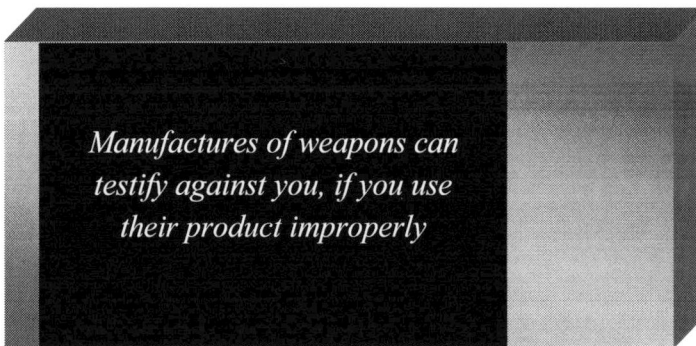

Manufactures of weapons can testify against you, if you use their product improperly

weapon may send their expert witness to testify on your behalf, in court. This is a good thing, everyone is on your side you did what you were supposed to do, when you were supposed to do it.

But, if you use one of the non- common weapons, the manufacturers will not back you. The manufacturer of the Magnum flashlights have said they do not condone the use of their flashlight as an impact weapon. They will not testify on your behalf and will not back you in a use of force lawsuit.

The manufacturers the tasers have required training every year for the officers that use their product. If your department does not comply

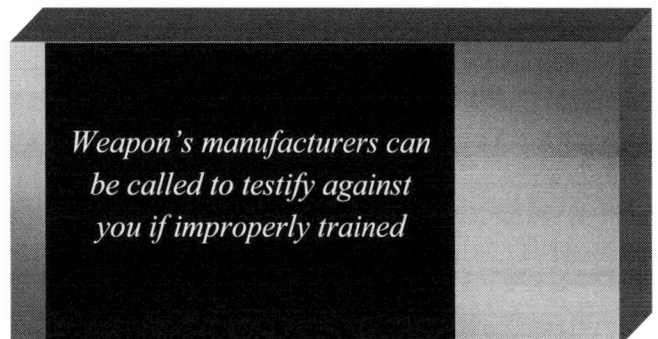

Weapon's manufacturers can be called to testify against you if improperly trained

with the required training every year, the manufacturer will not back you, or your actions.

If these manufacturers are not testifying on your behalf, who will they testify for? The defense! The bad guys attorney can and probably will hire the manufacturers expert witnesses to testify against you. This is a bad thing.

This is why is it so very important to document that your use of a non-common weapon was purely and strictly a self defense, reaction to the bad guy attacking you.

Try to avoid these non-common weapons if you can, and stick to the issued, trained and certified weapons you are familiar with and have trained with.

However, if it does happen and you apply the ticket book to the bad guy as he is coming at you, here is how you write it up.

Police Report

Investigation:

,,,During the traffic stop, I began to write out a traffic citation for the defendant.

The defendant began to argue with me and began to approach me. As he approached me I observed him throwing his sunglasses down on the side of the road.

The defendant then said he "was going to kick my ass into next week". I took a step backward as he lunged at me. I placed both hands up to try to re-direct the defendant. As I put my hands up to defend myself, my ticket book struck the defendant on his chin.

The defendant immediately stopped, dropped to his knees and placed his hand under his chin.

The defendant received a 1" long cut to the bottom of his chin. He was placed into handcuffs and taken immediately to the emergency room. He received 9 stitches and was released.

The defendant was then issued his traffic citations and taken to booking.

Some people just do not think these things through.

If your use of force involved the use of a departmentally issued, fully trained and certified weapon, here is how you write that up.

Police Report

Investigation:

,,,During the traffic stop, I began to write out a traffic citation for the defendant.

The defendant began to argue with me and began to approach me. As he approached, I observed him throwing his sunglasses down on the side of the road.

The defendant then said he "was going to kick your ass into next week". I took a step backward as he lunged at me. As I stepped back I threw my ticket book under the car and removed my ASP baton. I expanded my ASP baton and delivered two weapon strikes to the upper mass of defendant's left arm.

The defendant immediately stopped, dropped to his knees and placed his hand over his left arm.

The defendant was placed into handcuffs without further incident.

The defendant had a red mark on his upper arm where the ASP baton made contact. The defendant refused medical attention.

The defendant was then issued his traffic citations and taken to booking.

Deadly Force

And finally, we come to the absolute maximum use of force in a police officer's career, deadly force.

Contrary to popular belief, there is no absolute or clear cut action that a bad guy must commit, to allow an officer to use deadly force. And, deadly force does not necessarily mean the bad guy has to die.

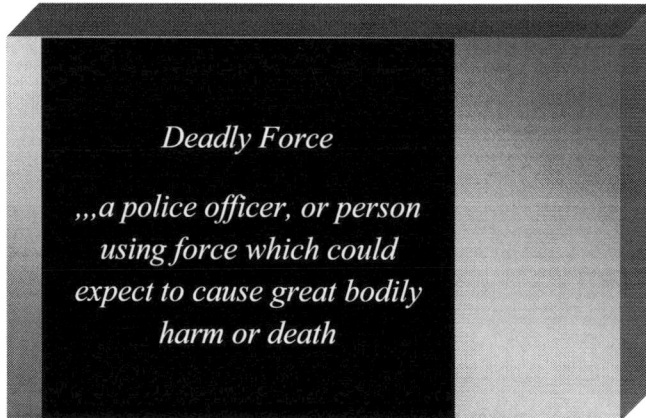

> **Deadly Force**
>
> *,,,a police officer, or person using force which could expect to cause great bodily harm or death*

Deadly force can be committed by using a deadly weapon, meant to kill.

Deadly force can be committed by using a non-lethal weapon in a manner meant to kill. Running your police car into someone. Hitting someone on the head, with a police baton.

Deadly force can be committed to defend yourself against an actual threat.

Deadly force can be committed to defend yourself against what you "thought" was imminent death. Someone points a piece of metal pipe at you, and it looks like a gun, you shoot first.

All justified, legal, lawful uses of deadly force, but you will have to explain yourself in each and every situation. And it is easier than you think.

What deadly force also includes

If you are involved in a deadly force situation, you will be a bit hyped up. Excited, spastic and you were scared, scared to death that you were going to die.

Remember that. If you did not think that you were going to die, or someone else was going to get killed, you may not be justified in using deadly force.

> *If did not you think you were going to die, you may not be justified in using deadly force*

You can **know** you are about to die because you are getting shot at, about to be rammed by a car or being thrown over a hood of a car, into interstate traffic.

You can **think** you are about to die because you told the bad guy not to move, but he removed a shiny piece of something from his waistband and started to point it at you.

You saw the bad guy pick up a baseball bat, put it on his shoulder and begin the motion of a swing at your partners head.

You have to know it, or you have to think it, and then you have to be able to say the all important statement, **"I thought I/he was going to die".**

Get ready to go on defense

This is the area of police work where you are going to get the most criticism. You will probably get sued, just because. Dead, bad guy's families sue police departments for a violation of the bad guys civil rights. Specifically, a violation of his 6th Amendment right to a trial.

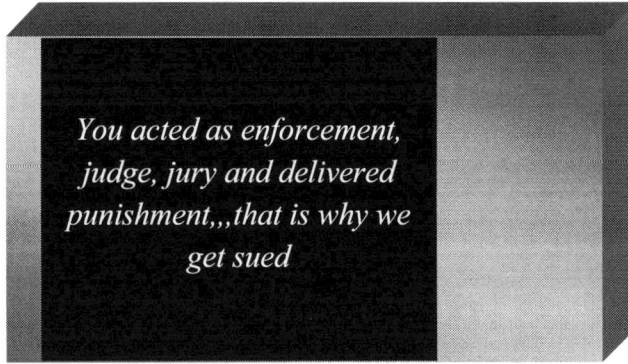

Here's why. The United States Constitution guarantees the right to a speedy, public, trial of the accused with the ability to face an accuser, cross examination, judges all of it.

What you did, as a police officer was

> *You acted as enforcement, judge, jury and delivered punishment,,,that is why we get sued*

see the bad guy committing a crime. You acted as enforcement, judge and jury and, without a trial you determined the bad guy was guilty of a crime and rendered his punishment on the spot, you executed him.

The fact that it was self defense and the bad guy was trying to kill you, right now, and the bad guy started it and the bad guy was totally wrong in every way, is irrelevant. You did not give him a trial, you get sued.

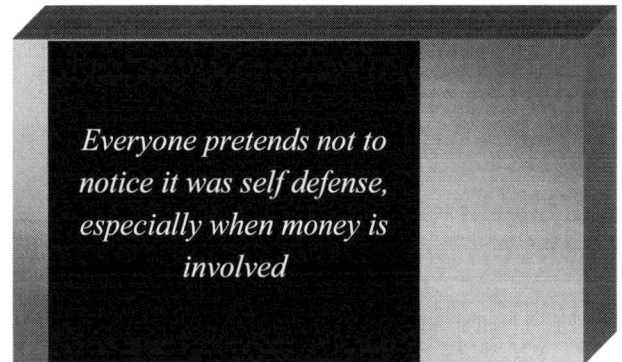

> *Everyone pretends not to notice it was self defense, especially when money is involved*

Why will you get sued, what is the point? Money. Dead, bad guy's attorney's want to sue someone to get lots of money for the family. You are not really who the attorney is after. The person or entity with the most money is actually the city or county you work for.

Your personal liability

You will be at the bottom, the beginning of that chain. Starting with you, the next entity to get sued will be your department, then the city or county you work for and probably the equipment manufacturer of the weapon you used.

This is called vicarious liability. You get named as a defendant, but you personally do not have to write a check for damages because you acted in a lawful manner. You used departmental issued weapons in an approved manner, with all the up to date training and certifications to prove this.

The courts just step on you as part of the process, to get to the deepest pockets.

Your training will be scrutinized. Your certifications will be scrutinized. Your conduct at the scene will be scrutinized. Your radio transmissions will be scrutinized. Your weapon will be inspected. Your internal affairs investigation will be scrutinized.

If you screw up, you will write a check

Then, your reporting of the incident will be scrutinized.

This will need to be the best police reporting of your career.

If you fail in any of the above scrutiny, then you could be named personally and assessed punitive damages. That means you do write a check to the dead guy's family.

If you don't have the cash, your kid's college funds will be fine. Not enough there? Pension, hand it over. Sell your house to raise the rest, that's fine, they'll wait.

What do you do to protect yourself

Now that I have scared you to death, let's look at how we can work to soften this, defend yourself and hopefully alleviate this lawsuit thing all together.

Like you just read before, you have to know you are about to die or you have to think you are about to die. Then you have to explain your thinking or reasoning to everyone else.

Your explanation will be in two ways. It will be verbal and it will be in writing.

Secure the scene

The verbal will begin at the scene. If you are involved in a deadly force situation, first secure the bad guy. Just because you shot him does not mean the threat is over. He can still pick up his gun and shoot you back.

Once he is secured, yes I mean handcuffed here, remove his weapon and secure it in any way you can. Hold it, hide it, do something with it so it cannot be picked up by someone else and used on you, or disappear from the scene.

Call for help

Then call for assistance. He is going to need an ambulance, you are going to need help and you need it all now. Take a deep breath and calm yourself just a bit so you can be understood. You need to sound calm, clear headed, authoritative, rational and in total control of the situation. Notify the dispatcher that you have been involved in a deadly force situation, give your location and immediately request an ambulance for the bad guy. This fact will be documented.

The radio transmission will be marked at this exact time, and documented. This transmission is the one that gets the firestorm started.

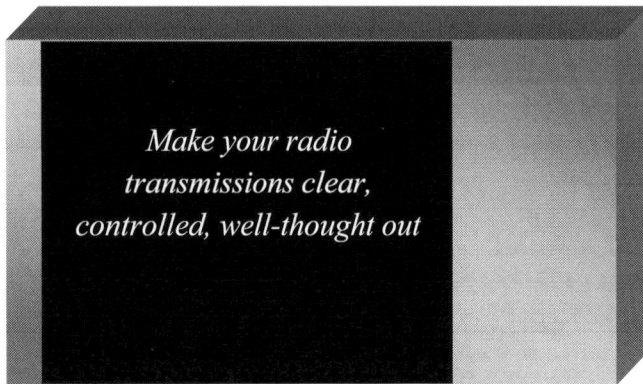

Make your radio transmissions clear, controlled, well-thought out

Notify the dispatcher of your injuries or of the fact you are not injured too. Your department will probably have all this protocol down already as policy. For your protection, do these things yourself, just to make sure they get done and their requests are documented on tape permanently. Then stay with the bad guy. Render aid, because you will document that you did, to the best of your abilities.

If you need back up, request it and say why, crowd is forming, you are injured, heavy traffic on the highway. Let everyone know what you need.

Again, calm, clear, concise voice transmissions and very clearly in control of the situation. You do not ever want to sound like you were reckless, over-reacting or just plain losing it out there.

When your back up arrives, have them secure the scene, the perimeter. Use the crime scene tape and tape it all up. This is now your crime scene, protect it.

If there is another threat, let these guys know about it, but do not start taking about the incident. Do not ramble, state stupid things or laugh.

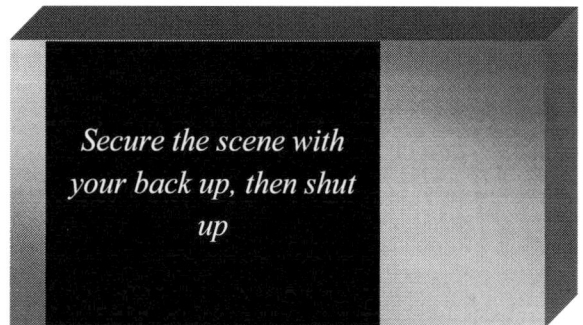

Secure the scene with your back up, then shut up

Keep your mouth shut and begin to organize your thoughts. If you say something stupid or anything that can be used against you, these guys may be called to testify against you. Don't make your buddies testify against you in anything.

So, who do you talk to? If you have a departmental union representative, talk to them. Many larger agencies already have this protocol in place too and they will be called to the scene, immediately for you. They are on your side, but they can testify against you as well if you did something illegal.

Now step aside and hand the investigation over

Your department will probably treat you as a victim. Meaning you will be interviewed by detectives, as a victim. Your interview will then be written out by that detective. You will probably be relieved of your weapon. This is for evidentiary uses and to count the bullets.

Organize your thoughts prior to speaking to anyone

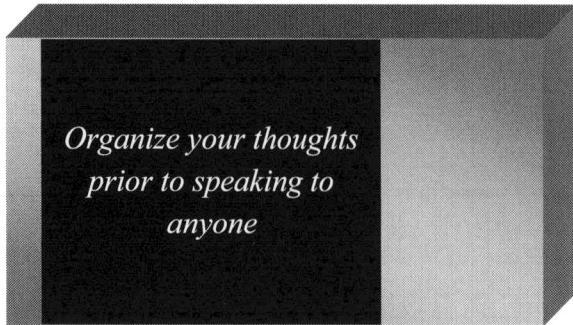

Give yourself time to calm down just a bit, organize your thoughts. Read over your departments deadly force policy. Not to condone what you did, but rather to brush up on terminology. Make sure you are using correct, departmental use of force, weaponry terminology.

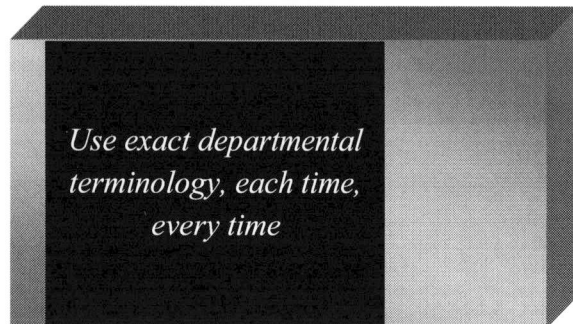

Use exact departmental terminology, each time, every time

Everything you say and do will be documented, but not by you.

When you are ready, take the detectives on a walk- through of the crime scene.

This is where you will tell them what the bad guy did, what you did in response and why you reacted the way you did. Use the term "I thought I was going to die". No one can tell you differently, if that is what you thought, then it is what you thought, period!

This part of the walk through will be quite easy, start at the beginning of the incident, chronologically and go from there. What you saw, what you heard, what you knew and what you thought, sound familiar?

Walk your investigator through the scene, chronologically

After the walk through is over, you will probably be required to put

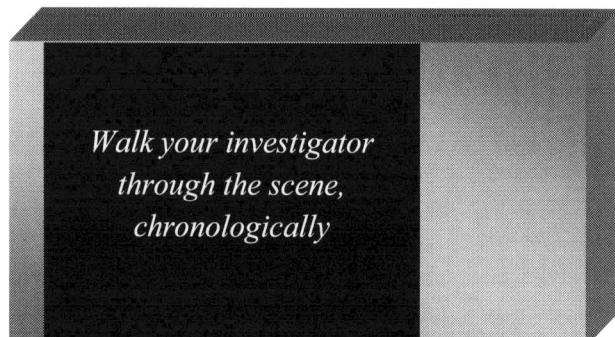

everything down on tape. An audible interview will done in a much quieter place. Usually, at the station. You will again go through the details of what happened.

This will be pretty smooth as well, you just did it on the street. Same thing, but now you are in a controlled, quieter environment. Everything you say will be on tape. It will be written out when you are done and used for, or against you.

Make it work in your favor. Again, use your exact departmental terminology. State again the exact moment you thought you were going to die.

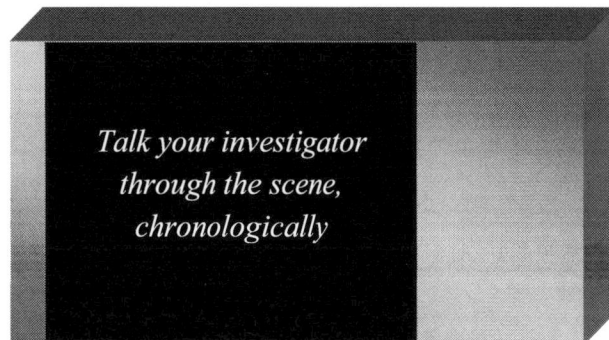

Talk your investigator through the scene, chronologically

If for any reason you begin to feel uncomfortable, or you feel the room is against you, or you feel like you are being harassed or interrogated, get your union representative to be there. No union rep? Call for an attorney. You are allowed by law to have an attorney, your department may not like it. They may even tell you you are not being charged with a crime. But, if during the interview you are read your rights, or told you are not free to leave, then it just became a custodial interrogation, protect yourself.

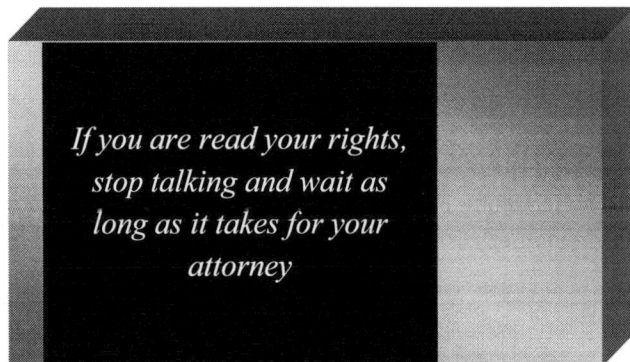

If you are read your rights, stop talking and wait as long as it takes for your attorney

If you need to take a break, take one. If they stall or don't let you, just threaten to throw up.

Just in case you have to write your own

Since you will probably be treated like a victim, your interview will be written by the detective that interviewed you at the scene during the walk through. You should not have to write out a report. But, if you are asked to write a report, no problem.

Here is what your deadly force report should look like.

Police Report

Details:

On the listed date and time, I was driving a marked police car west on E. Columbus drive. I had just passed the intersection of N. 21st street when I observed a known wanted person standing on the south-east corner.

This known wanted person was a white male, Samuel Johnston. I notified the dispatcher of my location and requested the suspect's name be run through NCIC to confirm a warrant. The warrant was confirmed by the dispatcher as being active for trafficking in narcotics.

I parked my police car on the north-west corner and got out on foot to watch the suspect and wait for my back-up unit to arrive.

As I approached on foot I heard someone yell "9". (common street term for notifying everyone the police are in the area) immediately I saw several people that had been loitering, begin to run in various directions. The suspect ran north on 22nd street, along the sidewalk. I turned to cut him off and was behind him, chasing him north on the west sidewalk.

I told the suspect to stop, he was under arrest. The suspect stopped, put his hand under his shirt, behind his back. I immediately ran behind a parked car.

The suspect removed a black revolver from his waistband and began to move the gun horizontally across his body in my direction.

I told the suspect to, "police, drop the gun", "police, drop the gun now".

The suspect looked directly at me and pointed the gun at me. I removed my weapon from the holster and began to point my weapon at the suspect. I observed a muzzle flash from the suspects gun and heard the sound of a single gunshot.

I discharged my weapon 2 times to stop the suspect from shooting and killing me.

Both of my rounds struck the suspect in his center mass of his chest. He immediately dropped his gun and fell to the ground. I approached him on foot and placed him in handcuffs. I moved the gun several feet from his reach, under a trash can lid, so it would not be picked up.

Police Report

Details Cont.:

I immediately notified the dispatcher of the fact that I had just been involved in a police shooting. I requested an ambulance, updated my location and had my supervisor notified. I requested additional units to respond as a back-up.

The suspect was breathing, shouting at me and said "I'm going to fucking kill you". The suspect had two bullet holes in his upper left chest. No exit wounds were found. I sat with the suspect, on the ground trying to hold him still. The suspect continued to try to kick out at me, and tried to spit on me.

I applied direct pressure to his two chest wounds, with a t-shirt from a nearby clothesline. Fire rescue unit #4 responded and the suspect was transported, immediately to Mercy Hospital.

Once at the hospital, the suspect went into emergency surgery. The suspect was operated on by Dr. Lyons. The suspect was stabilized and admitted to the hospital under police guard. The suspect's bullets were removed and placed into evidence by Ofc. Garcia. Ofc. Garcia completed the charging instrument for the outstanding warrant. (see supplement)

Detective brown responded to the scene and took possession of my police weapon for processing. It was replaced with an identical Glock 9mm, temporary replacement. (see supplement)

Crime scene techs, Williams and Jones responded and photographed and processed the crime scene. (see supplement)

The bullet from the suspect's gun was found on the electric pole, approximately 2 inches above where the car was located, that I had gone to for cover. (see diagram) My shell casings and the suspect's gun were retrieved and placed into evidence by our crime scene techs.

I received no injuries during this incident.

Intent

And finally, the last area that I would like to discuss is your intent. You can have all the best training in the world. You can have great weapons and use them proficiently. But, with the variables of human vs. human, with everybody in motion, there are bound to be mistakes.

You should not, and probably will not be penalized for mistakes, made in good faith. These types of mistake could be as simple as something like:

You set yourself up to deliver a weapon strike to the upper mass of the suspects arm to keep him from hitting the police officer on the ground. When you delivered the strike, *the suspect suddenly moved his arm and your police baton glanced off of his arm, striking his left temple area of his head, rendering him unconscious.*

On the outside we see, you just hit a guy in the head with your police baton. That is deadly force!

Not exactly. You didn't mean to. That was not your intent. Your intent of a weapon strike to the upper mass of the arm was totally justified use of force.

Hitting his head, was an accident.

The fact he is now unconscious, accident.

His head injuries, accident.

Do not try to cover these types of things up. Do not lie. Even though it looks bad from the outside, state your intent and defend your actions.

Writing out a use of force police report, or narrating an interview gives you the opportunity to tell your side of the story. It gives you the ability to explain not only your actions, but your reasoning as well.

Use this format to explain in great detail about what you did, felt and meant. There will be lots of people coming in behind you trying to un-justify your actions, but the fact remains you were there, they were not.

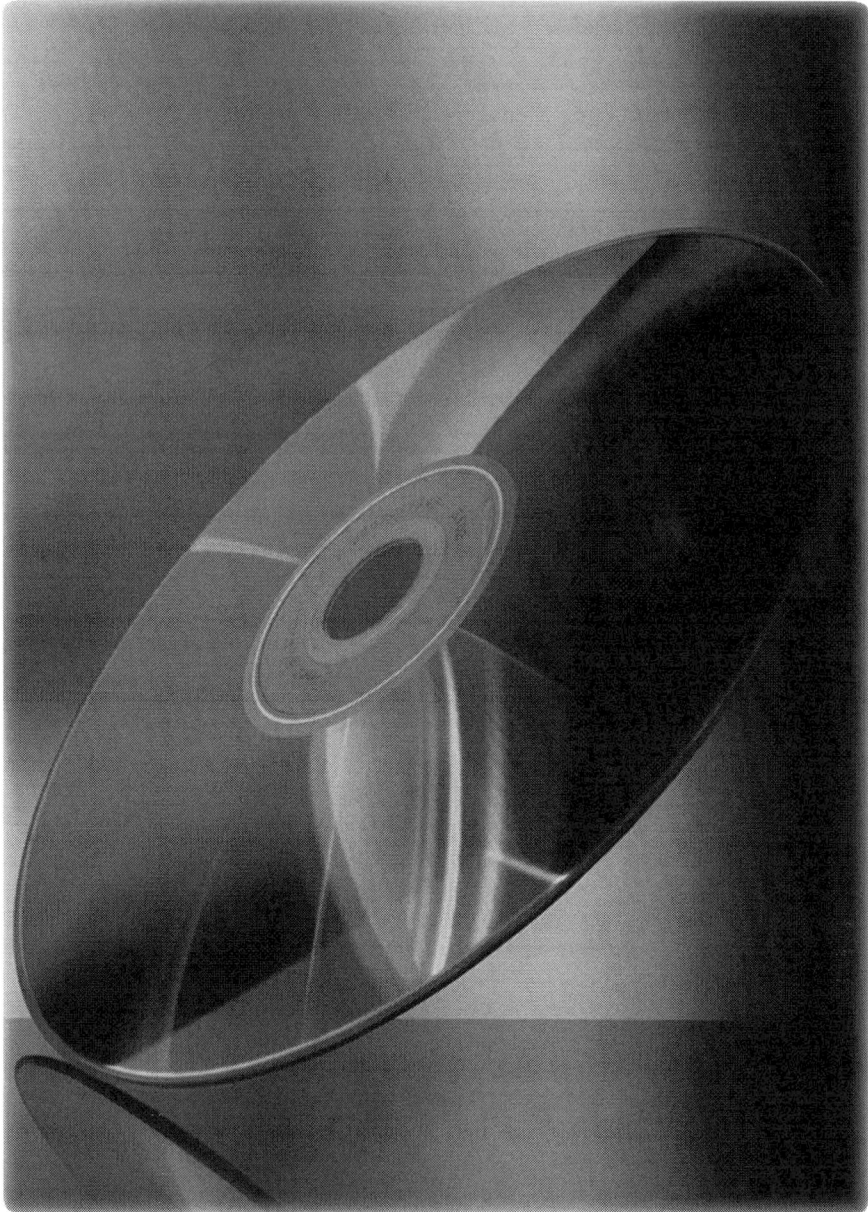

Chapter 8

Technology in Police Work:

The Geek Chapter

When I wrote my first book, this was in interesting and relevant, new subject. Now, this is an old subject. Technology is everywhere, used by everyone, for everything. The most common device is the computer. They are at work, home and school. Their endless uses and applications are pretty much understood.

As a result of this common use and ownership, there is a whole new type of criminal that has developed. Cyber crimes, computer crimes, theft and internet, deviant viewing are a whole new realm of crime.

Instead of trying to go into computer crimes, which is vast, we will focus on computer uses in law enforcement. Ways you can use a computer to make your job easier.

In law enforcement, computers have been used for a very long time, but not every person had access to them.

Computers at the station

Records

In the police station, records clerks kept copies of police reports in a computer database. The data entry was extensive, labor intensive and subject to human error. Reports were also scanned into microfilm, to be mass stored for retrieval later.

Everything was on an internal network with its own programming being written, usually by in house programmers, on an as needed basis.

Dispatch

Dispatchers used to use a card system to take dispatch calls. They would take a call from its first telephone complaint, fill out a card, the card was handed to a dispatcher who voice dispatched the call to an officer. The card was stacked, systematically so the dispatcher knew who was out on what call. The dispatcher was able to check on the officers periodically for safety reasons, the card was filed away, when the officer came off the call.

This card method is still being taught today. In the case of an extreme emergency, complete system wide, computer crash. We still need to know where all the officers are.

Just about every agency has a dispatch system where the calls are sent via a computer in an internal network system. Calls are voice dispatched and calls are computer dispatched.

Bad guy's criminal backgrounds can be checked simultaneously as the call is being sent, cars checked as stolen too. The officer is well informed, before they even arrive at a call.

The programming

Most agencies use computers that have a Windows based operating system. Some do not. A few years ago, some enterprising programmers created and sold programs that were thought to address law enforcement's needs.

These programs included report writing, archiving, and almost paperless systems of editing, reviewing and storage. These programs included dispatch systems with everything from calls for service to saving voice transmissions of every radio transmission made.

The price tag for these programs was significant. It had virtually no competition and agencies that wanted to be paperless and current and considered technologically advanced, had to buy into these programs.

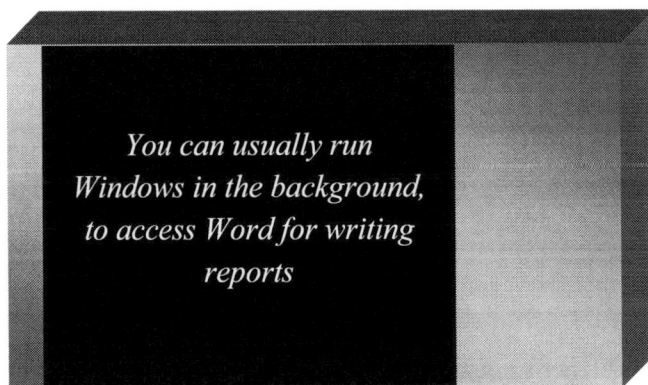

You can usually run Windows in the background, to access Word for writing reports

However, these programs were very limited in their ability to expand and be compatible with other systems, including Windows. The time these first programs were being developed, Windows was just so-so. Now Windows is everywhere, it is the mac-daddy in operating systems. The most recognized, easy to use system with updates, compatibility and endless expansion capabilities.

Some lucky, smaller agencies that could not afford the first generation programming are stuck with Windows, hah! Some of the bigger agencies that have the older programming are stuck, spinning in place.

This book is being written using references to Windows based operating systems. Hopefully you will get to use it at your agency.

I have discovered that many officers that use older programming also have Windows operating systems running in the background. They are able to access the word processing programs for spell check, cut and paste, downloading photos and so on.

They also have internet connections in their cars and have access to an unlimited amount of information at their fingertips. Just hope it is your fingertips as well.

Computers in police cars

Calls for service

A computer in your police car is an awesome toy. If you have an internet connection, your uses are limitless.

Your most standard use will probably be receiving calls for service. You can receive calls from the dispatcher. You can also take calls, as you will be able to see calls waiting for an officer to become available. If you are in training, this will give your training officer the ability to see which calls they want you to practice on, and take those calls next.

Your location, while out on a call will be monitored, but your time out at a call will also be monitored. Your supervisor will probably watch this closely.

Report writing

Once you are finished with a call, you can use your computer to write the police report for the call. This book leans toward you having a Windows based system with Word built in.

If your agency has a Windows based system, but does not have Word, usually due to budgeting or licensing issues, there is a company that can help your agency out with that.

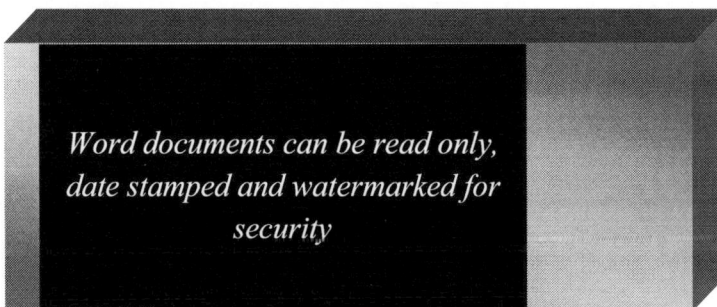

Word documents can be read only, date stamped and watermarked for security

Aleir, report writing and dispatch programs, by Automated Police Systems , Inc. is a company that has created a Windows based software program for law enforcement. This company specializes in providing software for the smaller agencies. They can even customize the software for individual agencies needs. Check them out at Aleir.com.

Microsoft Word is a word processing program that many are already familiar with. Looks familiar, easy to use with a great spell check built right in. Word is so common that your reports will be able to be shipped to other agencies, even with photos attached and the reports can be opened and viewed by almost anyone.

You can protect your reports with watermarks and date stamps. Overwriting is not a problem either. Word has the ability to make your report a read only document, no issues with tampering or getting to court and finding add-ons you knew nothing about.

If your agency still handwrites reports, you can still use word to write the narrative. Just open a new word document, type in your heading, Interview or Investigation, type out the narrative, spell check it and save it. Then, when you are ready to print, just feed your agency's report form through the printer.

Photos and Video

Attaching crime scene pictures to your police report

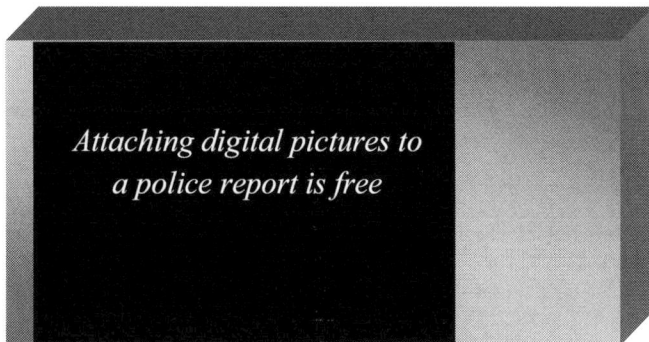

Attaching digital pictures to a police report is free

In the legal chapter we went over the guidelines for taking photos at a crime scene. What pictures can be taken, of whom were covered. Police officer's carrying their own digital camera now is no big deal.

Civilians carry their own cameras, camera phones and video cameras. They happily video us going about our day so they can run, not walk to internal affairs and try to complain on us.

There are many types of crimes scenes that can be photographed. Once the pictures are taken you can download them, as an attachment to your report.

Make sure that the photographs are an attachment, a separate file. If you simply download the photos onto the body of the report, they will be useless. Why is this? Most courts are not paperless. They need a photocopy of the original report. Photos added at the bottom of the report simply do not copy onto black and white, copied piece of paper.

Keep it as an attachment. Then anyone can open it on their computer. They can decide the value, and if the photograph needs to be printed. It can also be enlarged for depositions or court.

These attachments can sit as evidence, until needed, or shipped with the report to the prosecutor's office. Anyone else that needs access to the pictures can see them instantly.

The detectives can open the photos. You can have them properly printed, if needed for testifying in court. The prosecuting and defense attorney's can have them as well. Taking these photos will be invaluable for insurance companies when your complainant files a claim.

The best part is, the taking and attaching of these photos does not cost your agency a thing. As far as your investigative purposes, photos of crime scenes will be your most common use. If you are investigating a burglary and you have an unusual entry that left marks, or any other evidence lying around, photograph it.

Gang graffiti? Photograph it and ship it to your gang unit. Unusual weapons recovered? Photograph these and ship them to everyone. Drug arrests? Juries love to see the giant , blown up, original, crime scene photos of the clever hiding places or narcotics laid out on display. Did you have a civilian take photos of a live event? A photo of the suspect? Suspect's car?

Download these pictures directly into your car's computer, to attach them as a separate file to your report. Just to be sure to clearly mark the photos as coming from a civilian's camera and list the civilians as a witness in your report. They will need to be subpoenaed to possibly testify to the validity of the photos. Also, be sure to download the date/time/marker from the camera as well.

Can't download the witness' pictures from the scene? Have the person email the photos to your department email, as an attachment. Attach their file to your report, again marked as coming from a witness at the scene.

Your prosecutor can decide if the photos can be used, and they usually can get the photos in if the witness is available to testify.

Just remember to follow your department's policy for procedure of when to photograph, and state laws on what to photograph. This is an invaluable tool, not only for the convenience involved but for the preservation of evidence at your crime scenes.

Video of Crime Scenes

Do you have digital video of a crime scene? Today's digital, color recorders have come a long way from the old VHS recorders. Remember the black and white cameras, hidden in the fake stereo speaker behind the clerks head in the convenience store? That was considered very cool technology. A secret, hidden, video camera to record robberies.

The camera was either on a continuous loop, or the removal of bait money from the drawer turned the camera on.

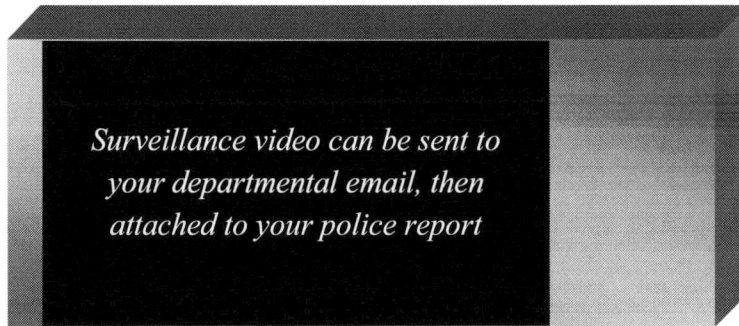

Surveillance video can be sent to your departmental email, then attached to your police report

All we, as police officers had to do was take a blank VHS tape to the store that was robbed. The store would make a copy of the incident for us. We had our own black and white, no sound, grainy copy of a grim reaper, werewolf looking guy, in a black hoodie. He was pointing what looked like a cooking implement, menacingly at the clerk.

These were the normal surveillance cameras, and they were usefull in identifying your bad guy. If he was the grim reaper, who wore a hoodie.

Now we have digital surveillance technology. Another great little piece of technology, installed by various businesses for many reasons, not just crime prevention or identification.

At a cost of over 5 thousand dollars, for the cheapest systems, the businesses now have the equivalent of an employee who never sleeps.

They are used for loss prevention, employee honesty, liability and workers compensation claims. And, of course, recording a crime. But, a favorite part of this technology is the owner has the capability to watch their business, remotely from any other location, even home.

Keep this in mind when you respond to a call. You may be watched from any number of surveillance cameras, with every move recorded.

These cameras are completely digital. They have the ability to record and store 24 hour a day images, depending on the size of their hard drive.

These cameras usually have a very high line of resolution. This is perfect for the investigators to have the ability to enhance the photos for a close up of faces, even hands during questionable transactions.

These cameras can be put in every conceivable place. Some are wireless and run on a 9volt battery. Wires are no longer needed for camera placement.

These cameras are usually set up for a shot of the upper torso and face. This camera angle is specifically done for law enforcement purposes. If you are investigating a crime with digital video surveillance, ask to see the camera set for this angle. Stay away from the wide angle cameras, they do not allow for effective enhancements of the footage. Most of these cameras will have sound as well.

There are several ways you can get the footage from these cameras hard drives. The owner can email you the video clip to your departmental email. And you can add it as an attachment. But, this only works on files that are fairly small. 5GB is about the max for this.

If the file is larger have the owner burn a copy onto a CD/DVD for you.

This CD/DVD would then be placed into evidence with an entry on your report as to its existence.

If you want an immediate picture for your report, have the owner email you a still shot of the best frame, to your department email. Attach that to your police report for further use.

In addition to the entry of the CD/DVD on the report, remember to put in the report that the original recording has a watermark. If the recording has one, it shows the recording cannot be tampered with. But, always include the person who provided you with the recording, in whatever format provided. They will be listed on your report as a witness. This will be important when your case goes to court. The recording is a piece of evidence. Having a solid, complete chain of custody of this piece of evidence ensures it can be entered into court.

As far as treating a business' video recording as evidence, treat your car's recording as evidence as well. If you are downloading the footage wirelessly or taking in your flash drive, if the footage is going to end up in court as evidence, treat it as evidence.

Accessing NCIC

Another great use for a computer in the police car is running a bad guy's name. This will be done on your department's program or operating system, even teletype. You will have access to NCIC (National Crime Information Center) a database created in the mid 1960's for a uniformed crime information storage and retrieval system.

> *If it has an identification number, it is probably in NCIC*

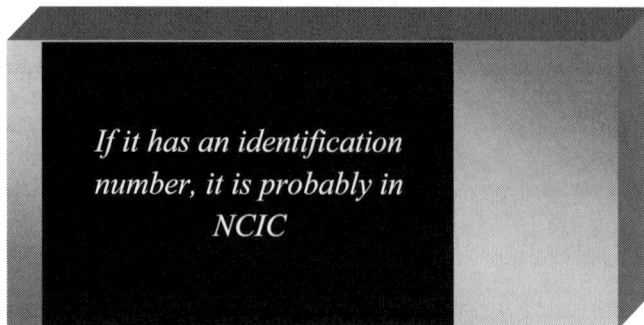

Due to the massive database of the NCIC system, you can also look up missing persons, stolen guns or other property with a serial number. Stolen cars, stolen tags, unidentified bodies. There are currently more than 17 files that contain over 10 million records. All accessible to you, as a law enforcement officer.

The database is maintained by the FBI, but information is taken in from any authorized police agency. Therefore, only the same police agency that submitted information can remove that information from the NCIC database.

That is known as placing a pick-up or warrant. If found, recovered or solved, cancelling a warrant or "hit" can be done from your car too.

Instant Messaging

On your home computer you probably have instant messaging capabilities. This is usually through your internet service provider or your email. These commonly are AOL IM or Yahoo IM.

You can do this from your car too. You can have a conversation with another officer, the dispatcher or your sergeant. But, keep in mind, if you are working on a private network system, and you most likely are, your conversations are not private!

You have no expectation of privacy, no right to privacy at all. That is the law, it has been tested, don't even go there. If you are making a date with a dispatcher, and this type of interaction has been prohibited, you will get nailed. The conversations cannot be deleted either even if you think you did.

Don't insult the dispatcher, don't get snippy with your sergeant, unless you simply do not care and you like saying, "you want fries with that?".

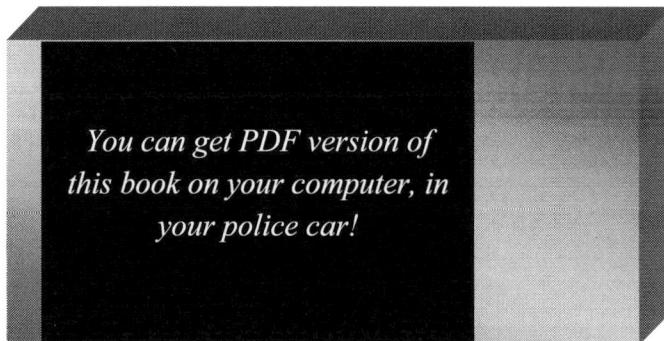

You can get PDF version of this book on your computer, in your police car!

Storing reference books

When you are in the academy you will probably be given a big, heavy book of current state statutes for your state. These statutes are also available on-line from every state. If your car has an internet connection, you can look up these statutes fast. You can also look up statutes by element and see what comes up, if it is a weird case, like "Trafficking in dead bodies". Misdemeanor in many states.

Most departmental policy books are available in an on-line format too. These are usually in PDF format. They look and act just like a book. So a search engine is probably not available. But, if you have an index, there is usually a counter on the side to show page numbers.

You can even have this report writing book in the same PDF format, downloaded into your car. For reference reading, refreshing, boring late nights, or just to hog up some memory.

Public access websites

If you have internet access in your car there are a few websites you may find useful. Not specifically law enforcement, these are websites that contain pubic information. These are websites of county records. Such records are court filings.

You can even get into your property appraiser or tax assessor's office to find out owner's information on property, names and additional addresses.

Invaluable to you if you are working on drug cases and need real property owner's info on rental homes, or tactical calls on homes. Really, anything where you need all the background on an address or location. It is all public. Available 24 hours a day, beats waiting for business hours to go to the crowded courthouse.

Look with a webcam

Another great use, if your car has internet access is the ability to look around town on various webcams. These webcams are predominately popular in tourist areas.

Some are monitored from a nearby location, recorded and some of them are archived.

If you have a large, expansive social area, or a row of bars, there is probably a webcam. Many popular bars have them inside too. The cameras point at the band, but some point at the crowd. Useful if you need to take a peek inside a bar without the uniform being seen.

Most major cities have webcams for traffic areas. These traffic cams are usually news agency related cams. They point to nasty intersections so people can monitor traffic prior to going to work. No reason you can't take a peek too if you need to see how a particular intersection is looking.

Some businesses have wireless cams for security. If you are close enough and you have Windows media programs, you can access and look through the business cameras. These are even being used by neighborhoods that have crime or drug problems. Private citizens have set up these cameras so a nearby officer can go on and watch the street for drug activity, all without being seen by the bad guy. Again, public video, no search warrant needed.

Computers in a police car are a tool we simply cannot live without, this is just scratching the surface of what you can do to get, and stay connected to what is going on around you.

Microphones and dash cameras

TV shows are loaded with footage from these. Its first uses were to document drunk drivers. Both their driving and roadside sobriety tests. Then they expanded, or exploded and are everywhere. They record everything in front of the lens, including what is being said.

It all gets recorded, the good and the bad. Remember this, enough said here.

Facial recognition software

High hopes for a software program that was not producing results. Facial recognition software takes measurements of key areas of the face creating a unique template.

This technology was supposed to be used to create a database of known bad guys, then recognize them when they went into a high risk environment.

Airports wanted to recognize people on a terrorist watch list. Casinos wanted to recognize card counters. Law enforcement overall, wanted to use it for surveillance.

Since the results were so disappointing, several major metropolitan cities took the software out of their systems completely. A high fail rate in airports has personnel using old fashioned methods, they look at someone.

The problem seems to come from the original photograph being shot at odd angles with bad lighting creating a facial shot that cannot be duplicated, therefore matched for later.

Worth more research here. But, not a favorite nor highly depended on method for law enforcement. (USA, Today, 2007)

Gps Cell Phone Tracking

Lately we have been hearing a lot about the use of the GPs tracking of a person via a cell phone. This is a great little piece of technology for law enforcement. It essentially allows the police to conduct a surveillance of the suspect, real time or even delayed.

How does this work? If a bad guy is carrying a cell phone, and it is on, it can probably be traced. On means just that, "on". It does not have to be in use, the bad guy does not have to be constantly talking for this to work.

There are currently two different ways to access the tracking feature in a cell phone. The first is by using the triangulated radio signal from a cell tower. This uses the cell phone, "ping" to find out where the cell phone is, or was. It is accurate for finding a cell phone from 3 to 300 square miles, depending on the tower.

The next method is using the E911 system. This was created for safety reasons. The "on" cell phone sends a signal to a satellite from your cell phone GPS chip. This little bit of technology is accurate in pinpointing the phone within about a 30 foot range.

Nice huh? Most cell phones have this technology silently built in.

The technology is not accessible to just anyone. Cell phone companies are now requiring interested parties come to them with a search warrant. Smart for the cell phone company since tracing someone's movements does raise issues with Fourth Amendment rights advocates.

Law enforcement has been accessing this information for years by getting subpoenas from judges, and giving the cell phone companies the court orders.

However, previously the warrants were loosely stating. "criminal investigation", or "ongoing investigation", type of requests. Many state supreme courts have begun refusing such requests and not granting a subpoena for the cell phone information. Instead, the courts have been requesting the subpoena come to them with probable cause, more than reasonable suspicion, for a court order to be granted. These judges are even publishing opinions based on their reasons. They are trying to legislate from the bench in the absence of strong federal or state laws.

What this means for you, during your investigations is this. Get the subpoena, based on probable cause the first time, get it right.

Using this technology for safety reasons or missing persons does not require a subpoena. This is especially true in an emergency situation. But, if you are conducting an investigation and you need back tracking of the cell phone user's actions, get that subpoena properly the first time.

In your report you would write in the investigative section that you obtained a subpoena based on probable cause. Document what that probable cause is, in great detail.

Using this technology is invaluable to law enforcement, but it's like any other new technique. Police are seen as abusers or potential abusers. We truly have no interest in tracking the moves of the everyday citizen. Way too boring. There are so many bad guys to keep an eye on, who really cares about Joe the Plummer anyway.

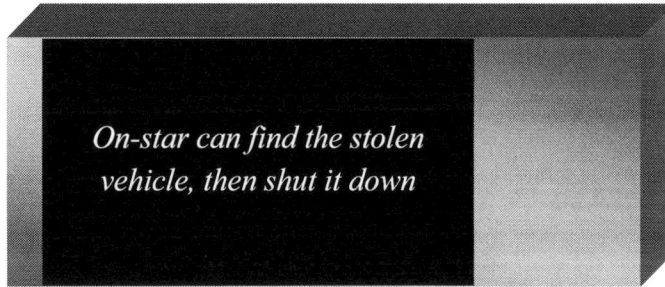

On-Star

Don't forget, "On-Star" uses the same GPS tracking technology. If you are conducting a stolen auto

On-star can find the stolen vehicle, then shut it down

investigation, ask if the owner's car has On-Star. If the car is equipped with it, call On-Star on the phone. Their system can pinpoint the car immediately. Most systems even use direction and wheel speed to pinpoint the vehicle even better.

Once the car's location is pinpointed, have your department's units head toward it. When your units are close enough, On-Star will remotely shut the car down!

On-Star will remotely turn off the accelerator, the car will slow to no faster than 5mph. Steering stays intact, braking still works, they just can't go any faster. Can you imagine how surprising for the bad guy and how much fun for us this can be?

Ask the complainant about On-Star for missing person's reports and stolen auto reports. Since it only requires a phone call to the On-Star service, it is even quicker for locating a complainant's car than a cell phone GPS.

Write in the investigative portion of your report that you accessed the On-Star Service during your investigation.

Amber Alert

The Amber Alert Program is a voluntary partnership between law-enforcement, broadcasters, transportation agencies and the wireless industry. This program acts to activate a statewide bulletin in child abduction cases.

The goal is to notify as many people as possible through a variety of mediums, of the crime, the description of not only the bad guy, but the missing child as well.

A.M.B.E.R. from America's Missing Broadcast Emergency Response. Was made possible by the 2003 PROTECT Act being signed into law. This law strengthened law enforcements ability to investigate and punish offenses committed against children.

The tragic incident of the abduction and murder of 9 year old Amber Hagerman, in 1996, prompted the legislation and subsequent development of the AMBER alert system

For our purposes you will be notified, as a law enforcement officer, by computer or dispatcher of a child abduction in your jurisdiction. But, all around you are citizens that have been notified as well. They may be looking for the suspect, child or suspect's vehicle along with you.

The general public receives this information from the new overhead, lighted, highway signs, radio broadcasts, even live email streaming.

If you are investigating an abduction of a child, you as law enforcement can place the missing child into this system for your investigation as well.

When you receive the information about the abduction and take the description from the complainant, notify your supervisor immediately. Statistics show most children that are abducted by a stranger are murdered within three hours of the abduction. Time is very important here.

To access the AMBER alert system there are a few criteria that need to be satisfied first.

A.M.B.E.R. Alert Criteria

- Confirm the abduction
- Is there a legitimate risk of injury or death?
- Is there enough of a description (child, suspect, vehicle)
- Is the victim within the age range for your state?
- Place a pick up in NCIC

Know your states laws on the minimum age. Each state is different, ranging from 17 to 14 as the minimum age. If you are near a state line, send your AMBER alert information to the neighboring state. Each state has signed an agreement, as part of the legislation to agree to post all requesting state's AMBER alerts.

When you are writing your police report, you would write in the investigative portion of the report your actions. If you placed the alert for the missing child, document the time you placed the NCIC pick up for the child and the time local media outlets were notified to place the alert.

If you are responding to a call regarding an already placed AMBER alert, document the alert details and who notified you directly. Dispatched notification or waved down by a citizen, whichever does apply.

Your agency will probably have a procedure in place regarding the investigation of AMBER alert complaints. If your city has an alert you may receive many false leads. Document these as you receive them. Listing all the witnesses information so they can be contacted later by detectives if needed. (DOJ, 2003)

For more information about the nationwide AMBER alert program or legislation:

http://www.amberalert.gov/guidelines.htm

Silver Alert

Mary Zelter, 86 of Largo Florida, checked herself out of a nursing home and went for a drive. Mary, suffering from dementia, accidentally drove into a waterway and drowned. Her daughter Mary Lalluci helped create the bill that would allow missing senior's information to be placed on the states AMBER Alert system.

The ability for placing a senior into the system is expanding rapidly, nationwide. Many states have already passed legislation to allow their AMBER Alert systems to be used in this manner. Other states are writing bills to modify their own laws now.

The criteria for placing a missing senior into the system is just as stringent as placing a missing child. This is kept fairly strict to keep the system from becoming diluted and announcements from becoming to routine.

SILVER Alert Criteria

- The person is believed to be suffering from dementia or other cognitive impairment, regardless of age
- The person is believed to be missing, regardless of circumstances
- A missing persons report has been filed to law enforcement
- The missing person has had a pick up placed into NCIC

Specific medical information is not to be distributed, to protect the missing person's privacy and to protect them from possible exploitation.

To place a Silver Alert for a qualified missing person, follow the same procedures for an AMBER Alert. When you initiate the report for the missing person, write in the investigating section your justification for placing the alert. Also, document your actions in placing the Silver Alert through your agency.

Reverse 911

The commonly known "Reverse 911" system is a telephonic notification system. The technology is from a private company called Reverse 911.

The technology, in the form of an actual dedicated computer terminal or software, or an agreement for the company to send emergency messages, must be acquired by each agency individually.

Does your agency have this technology? They probably do.

The system is commonly called reverse 911 and is used by police agencies, schools, college campuses and military, nationwide for quick, massive public notification of emergencies.

The types of emergencies that can go out on this system are, missing children, endangered adults, crime alerts, information on critical events and evacuations.

Recent successful uses are from the San Diego area where evacuations were required, due to wildfires. A recent critical event use was a small community in Tennessee, due to a potentially dangerous bear alert for the area.

The technology can be used for non-emergency as well. I regularly get notifications from my kid's school about PTA meetings, school closings and happy holiday wishes.

For emergency notification you are automatically included, if your land line phone number is listed. If your number is un-listed or you have a cell phone you would rather receive notices on, or if you have VOIP, you will need to register with the agency jurisdiction where you live. And if you are in a neighboring community, you can register for that jurisdiction too.

This technology has received a tremendous amount of media attention from it uses on college campuses. Quick texting has been implemented in those areas. It is basically the same technology, but it requires a text receiving database created completely by student's voluntary enrollment.

Since the tragic campus shooting at Virginia Tech, campuses have been scrambling to get on board with a simple, quick, unified system for emergency notification. Unfortunately Virginia Tech was not an isolated incident. Many shootings preceded this one and a few have followed. Due to the spreading nature of a college campus, single building lock-down methods are only effective building by building.

This is a reality and a hurdle to overcome. Group text messaging is being put into use on college campuses, nationwide. This seems a natural fit for college students. Most own cell phones. They carry their phones everywhere. Contacting an entire campus of an emergency should be simple, quick and very effective. However, this system is only as effective as the student enrollment.

Amazingly only about 30% of students, nationwide are participating in such programs. Schools closer to Virginia Tech are reporting higher enrollment numbers.

How this system works is quite straightforward. An emergency is reported to campus police, standard manner. The campus police can then send out a group text message alerting the students of an emergency, and what to do. Or, the campus police contact any number of private companies they may be contracted with, to send out the group text for them.

The messages can be sent to specific groups, faculty or student wide. The mediums sent can be text message, email, RSS feed or wireless PDA. Such messages sent can include; emergencies, weather, school events, school closings or class cancellations.

The cost for the service, usually a group fee is charged by the texting company, to the university. The time delay for the message to arrive to the students can vary widely and depends on each student's individual wireless provider.

If you are responding to an emergency call to a campus, check to see if a group text was sent out to the student body. Document the information in the investigation portion of the report.

All of the advances in technology are great. If your department's budget allows for it, technology can make you job easy and thorough. But there is a downside. Some of the technology is so new there isn't even legislation to govern its uses. This is where the police officer is expected to use prudent judgment.

Just because there isn't a law to cover it, doesn't mean we get to use, or do it. Basically if we, as law enforcement officers can look at another person, another person's stuff, freely and in the open, than it's ours. If it is abandoned, trashed it's ours.

But, if we have to even crane our necks to see it or them, climb a fence to see them, open a door or hack into any type of system to look at, track, see or monitor them, well we need legal permission.

Get your probable cause, get your subpoenas, and put your bad guy away properly.

The End

You have made it through a really long, dull subject. Hopefully you have a basic idea of how to organize yourself, gather information and put it down on paper. With a few months of practice this will become comfortable, quick, you will be really good. Do be patient with yourself. You are not expected to know everything, but do know how to look things up.

Each agency will add to what you learned in this book. Some will take parts away. Simply adapt to the individuals required elements. They will change a lot.

This is a fun, rewarding job. But we are the police, so we have to follow the rules. Even though no one else does. The most important part of police work, always is go home each night!

Samples, Samples, Samples!!!

Here it is the coveted chapter in police report writing books!

For the many years I was teaching, my students were constantly asking for samples they could look at, or refer too to help get things started. I refused to give them samples,,,why?! Well, because my lieutenant told me, while I was teaching, not to give out samples. He claimed giving out samples would corrupt report writing skills. The students would learn only one way to write reports, and if they had a bad sample they would learn only a bad way to write a report...?

Hmmm, since he was my lieutenant, I listened to him and did subscribe to this theory for a few years. I have since realized he was wrong. I no longer listen to lieutenants, I listen to my students, and you want samples!

This chapter is for you and here is how it works. First, you will read a story,,,*disclaimer each story is in no way depicting a real person either factual or true, blah, blah, blah.* The stories are meant to be humorous. Incidents are explained in great detail with some exaggeration. Why? Because this is boring stuff to have to read anyway, so I am going to make it fun. But, also to give you a great mental picture of the incident, which will make it more memorable.

First you will read the story, or incident for police service.

This style of call for service story, accompanying police report, written and put together for you, is continued for each and every type of offense.

After you have read a few of the stories and reviewed the accompanying reports you will begin to see a pattern emerge. Many of the beginning paragraphs sound alike. The order in which the report is constructed starts to look consistent. With the exception of the elements being switched around to match the crime, it does start to look alike.

That is perfect!! You are getting it, congratulations. This is the part, while teaching a classroom that I begin to see students visibly relax, I love this part!

You are building a police report one sentence or paragraph at a time. This method keeps your thoughts organized by allowing you to only write about one component of the crime at a time. You can pull all your details about this component from anywhere in your notes. This method will also help to jog your memory as to things you saw, but might not have thought to write down in your notes.

Just a quick thought before we begin, when you read these stories and accompanying reports, do not try to memorize these methods. Just read them and enjoy the humor. After reading a few, you will see the pattern emerge.

As you progress in your academy training or field training program, keep this book handy. Make your own notes in the blank spaces. Practice referring to this book to get you started. Soon you will not need this book at all.

My job is done, please remember to recycle.

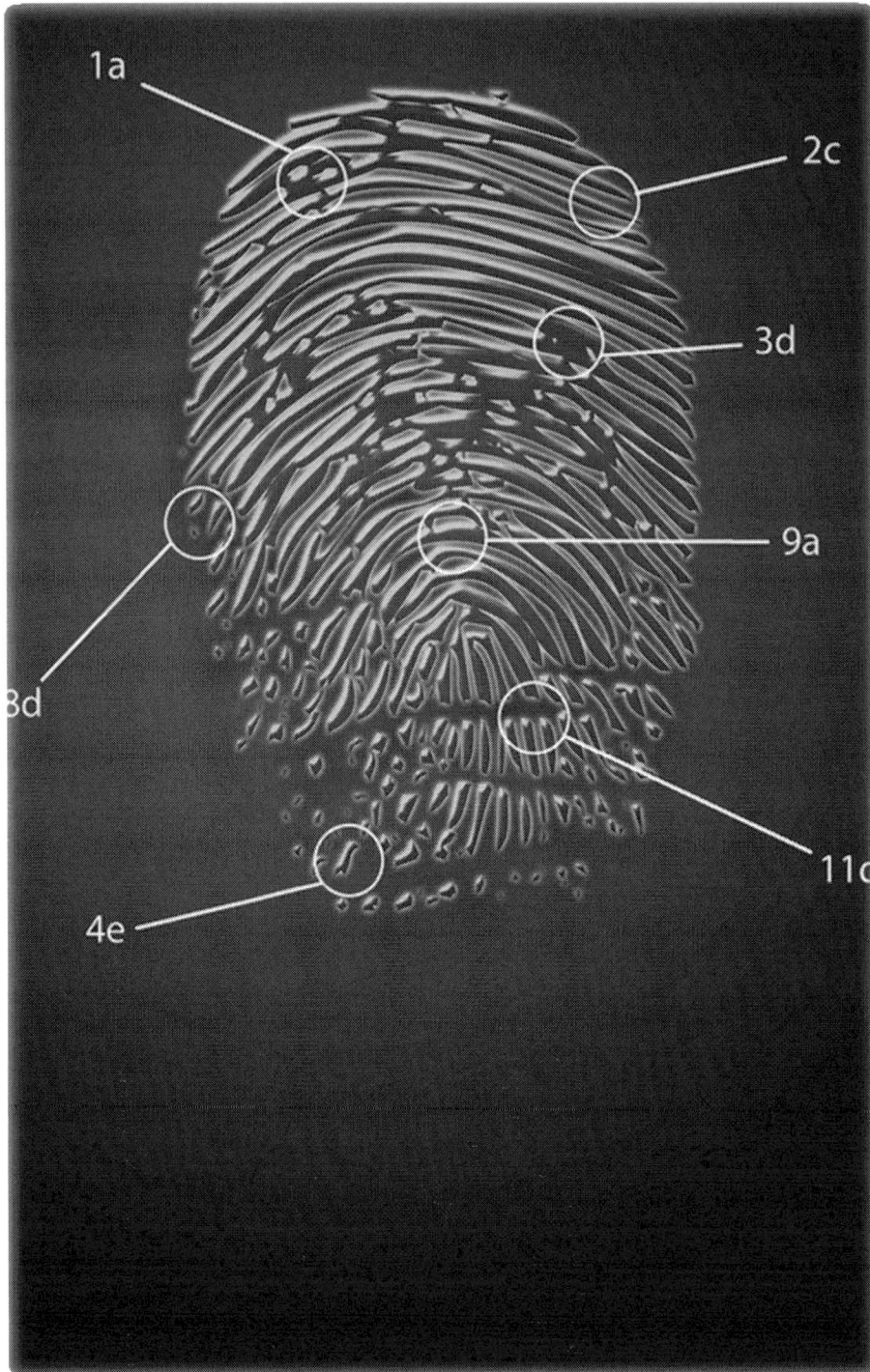

Burglary

Your dispatcher sent you a 911 call. A person on the phone said they were robbed and the line went dead. No answer on the call back. Since it was a 911 call with no call back or update, you will be treating this like an in-progress call.

The address from the call is a house. Parking your car about 3 houses away, you get out of your car, close the door quietly and walk toward the caller's house. When you are about one house away, a man comes out to the street and sees you. He runs up to you and tells you his house was robbed.

Stop here and get the preliminary information. Ask this complainant if the bad guy is still in the home. This complainant tells you no one is in the home, but his cat is missing.

Asking the complainant what happened, he tells you he just got home from work a few minutes ago. He parks at the back in the alley, walked in and noticed the kitchen door was already standing open.

This made him run in to look for his cat. When he was looking for his cat he saw a bunch of his things were gone. His freezer door was standing open too. He realized what was going on so he called 911 and ran back out to wait on police.

Since we are not sure how long ago this happened, we are going to go in, without the complainant and search the home for any suspects. After a quick search, we didn't find anyone inside. The freezer door was standing open, the food inside was almost defrosted.

Going back out to the complainant, we have him start with the last time he was home, and have him walk us through what he knows so far. The complainant said he left home this morning at about 7 to go to work, got back at 5. He doesn't know anything else.

Most of your interviews will go something like this. You will need to help the complainant understand what type of details you need, to conduct the investigation and try to put this crime back together.

This house is a single story, wood frame, bungalow style home. It faces east, toward the street. Along the sides of the home are older, rusted chain link fences. They are overgrown with bushes and vines. No one can see most sides of this house because of these vines. The back of the house leads out to the alley where the complainant usually parks his car. The rear door that was open, faces this alley. About the only traffic in this alley are other residents, that also use it to park.

Start with taking the complainant outside the home. Have him show you what is out of place. Look for items left in the bushes. Window screens lying on the ground. Tools left on the ground. Footprints, broken windows, clean spots on a dirty window sill, things like that.

What we find is there is a window screen lying under some bushes on the south side of the house. It just so happens this window faces a fence and you cannot see this window from the street because of the heavy, overgrown shrubbery. Perfect place for a bad guy to try to get in. No one can see you.

This window is a double-hung window. The top part of the glass is broken. This is broken right above the lock. The window is pushed up and opened all the way. On the outside window sill there is a slick coat of white paint. In this you can see a bit of heavy dust or dirt. There are a couple of smears on this dirt. It looks like someone or something scraped across this area. There are no fingerprints here, but it does look like someone might have boosted themselves up, across this sill and into this window.

The window is about 4 feet up from the level of the grass and leads directly into the living room. Looking around here, we don't see anything else that is out of place. We continue walking the complainant around the outside of their home. Everything else looks like it is in order.

Going inside, you start with the probable area where the suspect came in. the living room, next to the broken, open window. On the floor, under the window, there is a plant that is on its side, with dirt spilled out on the floor. Next to this plant, there is a console piece of furniture. The complainant said this was where his big screen TV set was sitting. Now there are a bunch of AV wires hanging out of the wall.

The complainant checks the rest of his house and notices there is a pillowcase missing from his bed. He also finds his checkbook has been taken out of his desk drawer. But, the checks are all still there. The complainant does not know why anyone would move things around and not take anything.

The only other weird thing is the freezer door was open. When you have the complainant check this, he realizes all of the frozen steaks are gone. Direct him back to the checkbook. Have the complainant go through the book, check by check. Very frequently the bad guy will only take a couple of checks from the center of the book. The complainant doesn't even know to report these, until after the checks have been cashed. Easier, less trouble for the bad guy since the checks were not known to be stolen and not reported stolen, until he is long gone with the money.

The complainant says there are in fact two checks missing from the middle of the book.

When he takes you into the kitchen, he shows you the door that was open when he got home. This door had a single cylinder lock. This is the type of lock that can be locked and un-locked from the inside, without a key. Easy for the bad guy to just open and walk out.

There does not seem to be anything else missing, or out of place. For all the items that are missing, you will need the brand, make, model, and serial numbers, anything that may identify the item. The quantity taken and the approximate, fair market value of the items.

The complainant's cat is still gone. The cat was a non-specific breed of cat, of no monetary value, but sentimental value.

You explain to the complainant about how cats are usually not stolen but rather it probably walked out when the door was left open, the complainant did relax just a bit. Next, you explain how steaks are actually very commonly stolen in burglaries (no we will not inspect grills in the area to see if the complainant's steak is being cooked). The pillowcase is usually used to carry all the stuff away, just like Santa.

Every area the bad guy could have realistically touched, is dusted for prints. I don't really believe in dusting non-condusive surfaces, just to say I did it, and lead the complainant into thinking it is actually useful. Instead, I like to explain to the complainant how the process works in real life.

We, law enforcement cannot dust for prints on every surface in your house. It is time consuming, messy and does not bring any results anyway. We do not bring in ultraviolet, infrared, heat seeking, DNA light equipment to find the single hair left on the floor by the bad guy. And finally, there is no machine on earth that we can pace that single hair into that will give us the home address, current photo and email address of the bad guy.

We dust for prints, maybe take a couple of pictures, talk to a few neighbors, check nearby pawn shops, go outside and call for the lost kitty and we leave.

All the statutory elements for a burglary of a dwelling are in place. We will write this report as a burglary.

Synopsis

An unknown suspect entered the compl.'s home, took the listed property, and fled, unseen, in an unknown direction.

Police Report

Investigation:

I received this call as a 911 emergency, by computer dispatch. On my arrival I met with and interviewed the complainant.

As I approached the compl.'s home, I observed it was a one-story, wood frame, single family home. The home was on the west side of the street and faced east toward N. 22nd st. The front door of the home faced east and was a glass etched, fiberglass door. This door had a double cylinder, dead bolt lock, which was intact.

The rear of the home faced west toward an alley. The south and north sides of the home were concealed from the view of the street and alley by heavy vines and tall shrubbery.

The rear door of this home was standing open and had an intact, single cylinder, dead bolt lock. This lock was un-locked.

On the south side of the home I located a double-hung window with a section of glass broken out. Under this window, on the ground was the window screen. This window was opened all the way up. The sill under the window had a clean smear in the dirt of the ledge.

Police Report

Investigation Cont.:

This window looked into the compl.'s main living room. Inside this living room the compl.'s big screen TV set, was removed. Across from this living room was the compl.'s bedroom. The pillow case and checks were removed from this room.

The compl.'s kitchen was located at the rear of the home. The freezer was located in here.

Serial numbers for the missing TV set were placed into NCIC. A stolen check form was completed and sent to the fraud unit.

I dusted all affected areas for fingerprints. Several prints were recovered from the doorknob. These prints were sent to the lab for processing.

Photographs were taken of the scene. They were downloaded and added to this report as an attachment.

I searched the immediate area for any additional evidence, or witnesses with negative results.

Interview:

Complainant,

The compl. Said he left for work this morning, his home was locked and all items, doors and windows were intact. When he came home in the afternoon the kitchen door was standing open and all the listed items were missing.

The compl. Has no idea who would come into his home and take anything. The compl. Does wish to prosecute if anyone is arrested for this offense.

Grand Theft Auto

Your dispatcher just sent you a call on your computer. A hysterical woman says her car is gone. She said she woke up about an hour ago to go to work, but her car is missing from the driveway.

The car is described as a 2004 Kia Amanti, silver with a Florida license plate of ABC 123.

Driving toward the complainant's home you watch for passing silver cars that may match the description of the complainant's car. When you arrive at the complainant's home you notice the complainant is outside her home waiting for you. She is very upset and crying.

You park your police car just before her driveway and walk to her at her home. As you walk up, you can see there is a large, dry square in the driveway where it looks like a car may have been parked. You remember a slight rain from earlier this morning. There are no obvious skid marks, tire marks or broken glass to indicate a broken window. There is no debris, no papers or trash lying near where the car was parked.

When you meet with the complainant she slowly calms down and you are able to begin an interview with her. You begin by asking her what happened (the easiest, non-threatening way to get a complainant to calm down and begin thinking).

The complainant tells you she went to bed last night at about 10:00 and knows the car was in the driveway because she turned off her porch light, and the car was still in the driveway. When she woke up to go to work she got ready and walked out her door at 7:00 and the car was gone.

Now, this is a pretty straightforward interview with not much to say as far as complainant's knowledge of the crime. What we will do from here is to try to narrow down a few details as far as when, and possibly who may have taken the car.

A few questions to ask the complainant are: Does anyone else have a key to the car? Has anyone told her they may take her car, angry boyfriend, father who co-signed for it? Is she current on payments?

Did she hear anything last night? There is no glass so the car window was probably not broken. But, could she have heard a wrecker re-possessing the car?

Next, does she keep any types of GPS devices in the car? Does she have a cell phone she may have left in the car? Any type of GPS, Garmin or anything similar? Does her car have On-Star, Lo-Jack or any other locating devices?

The complainant doesn't have any of that. Her cell phone is in her hand.

She tells you she has the only keys, no angry boyfriends or upset fathers to speak of. She is current on her payments and does not have any other ideas who could have taken the car.

Was the car left unlocked? This may account for her not hearing anything. Most complainants will tell you the car was locked. They mean to lock it, but can sometimes forget. Others will simply tell you they never lock their car door, they never need to. [I want to move there!]

During this part of speaking with, interviewing the complainant, we have pretty much determined who may have taken the car, absolutely no clue.

Next, we will try to get an idea of when it was taken. She already told us she knows the time frame of about 10:00 last night and 7:00 this morning the car was there, she did see it.

Let's try to tighten that up just a bit. Remember that dry spot on the driveway? You were working all night. It rained a bit at about 3:00 am, from your own estimation. If the car was there at 3:00, it kept the driveway dry, but was moved after that time.

Our time frame, by our own estimation just reduced to the car being taken between 3:00 am and 7:00 am.

Take down all the complainants' personal information. Along with all her vehicle's information. Here's a tip. Most people do not know their car's tag number by heart. An amazingly large number of people leave the cars registration in the glove box too. If they do not know the car's license tag number, look at their vehicle insurance card. This card has the vehicle identification number on it (VIN). It is usually in their wallet. Run this VIN number to get the tag number to complete the report. You will also need this information to place an alert and a pick-up (NCIC) on the vehicle later, during this investigation.

Ask the complainant about items that may have been in the car. Items such as her checkbook, credit cards? Many people leave a checkbook in the glove box. If so, she will need to have your police report number and contact her bank immediately to close the account.

Anything, like a laptop with her name on it, Ipod with her name engraved on it? Coin collection, her cat's Halloween costume? Document any type of item with identifiable serial numbers or unusual items that can be searched for in nearby pawn shops. Write it all down.

Did she keep a gun in the car? We will need all the information on the gun to place it in the computer as stolen (NCIC) and place a pick up on the gun.

Some may argue the gun should not be entered as stolen until the car is recovered and known for certain to be missing from the car. The car thief may never find the gun anyway, right?

Wrong. Wouldn't you, as an officer on the street want to know the stolen car you are behind, getting ready to conduct a traffic stop on, has a gun in it? This is information we need to know and we need to pass it along to all other cops.

If we get the car back and the gun is still inside, fine. We simply cancel the pick-up in the computer for the gun. But for now the car is gone, the gun is gone,,, stolen. Report it as such.

Since there is virtually no crime scene to process and we have all the information the complainant knows written down, we will branch out in our investigation a bit.

Looking around the driveway we see there is a house directly across the street that faces the complainant's driveway. This house has windows facing the complainant's driveway too. There are no other houses in the area that can see the complainant's driveway.

Walking over to the neighbor we knock on the door and ask to speak with the residents. You are able to legally inform the residents that a car was stolen. Using the narrowed time frame that you had already come up with, ask the resident if they saw or heard anything unusual during the night. Specifically that time, just after the rain stopped.

This neighbor said they sleep very soundly and heard nothing at all during the night.

Next, let's have this neighbor come outside and check his own car for signs of forced entry, damages or anything unusual. The neighbor checks his car but, everything seems normal.

You will need to get this neighbor's personal information. Even though he has no information to add, we did speak to him as part of our investigation. We will need to add him to the report just to let everyone reading the report later know that we did in fact check the neighborhood.

Finally, we return to the complainant. Give her a copy of the police report number on whatever form or card your agency requires.

Let her know she may be receiving a call at anytime day or night and have a friend on standby to bring her to her vehicle when we recover it. [about 95% of all stolen cars are recovered within 24hours] She should have a small portable gas can, full and handy. Put next to that a flat head and a phillips screwdriver. Just in case the police calls her in the middle of the night, it is hard to find those things while sleepy and in a rush.

Let the complainant know how the process works from here. Talk her through the task of the written report being created and also a pick up on her vehicle.

Taking a few extra minutes to let the complainant know the inside information of how things work realistically from here will put them at ease. They won't feel quite as helpless. They have a better impression of you and law enforcement and what to expect next.

All the statutory requirements are in place for a Grand Theft Auto.

Let's write this up.

Synopsis

An unknown suspect(s) took the complainant's car. The suspect(s) fled the area, unseen.

Police Report

Investigation:

I received this call via computer dispatch. On my arrival I met with, and interviewed the complainant.

On my arrival I observed the complainant's home was on the west side of the street. The driveway, where the car had been parked was a straight, clean, concrete driveway. This driveway was visible to one home, directly east, across the street. The driveway was also visible to the windows on the north side of the complainant's home. The driveway had no signs of broken glass, metal or any other type of debris.

After speaking with the complainant I met with a neighbor. This neighbor's car was checked for damages or signs of forced entry, with negative results.

The complainant was provided with a copy of the report number.

A BOLO was placed o the air for the missing vehicle with tag number.

A pick- up was placed in NCIC for the missing vehicle.

The immediate area was checked for the vehicle with negative results.

Police Report

Interview: Complainant,

The complainant said she went to bed last night at about midnight. When she got up this morning at about 7, her car was missing.

She said she is not late on any payments and no one else has keys to her car, the car was locked.

The complainant did not hear any sounds that she thought were unusual.

The complainant cannot identify any suspects regarding this offense.

The complainant does wish to prosecute if there are any arrests made regarding this offense

Interview: Neighbor,

This neighbor said he went to sleep at approximately 9pm. He heard no unusual noises during the night.

He said his vehicle is intact with no signs of forced entry or damages.

He cannot identify anyone reference this offense.

Recovered Stolen Automobile

Its late, you are about to go home. You see a car, parked with the lights on, in the middle of a field. Oh, great, you know what this is. It is a dump off, or there is a body inside. Hopefully it's just the dumping of a stolen car.

Through your computer you let the dispatcher know what you just found and have them send a midnight unit to relieve you. You get off in about 6 minutes.

Turning into the back of the field, you drive up behind the car, with your headlights off. The nearby street lights light up the car so you could see there is no movement inside.

The street lights are coming from the grocery store parking lot at the south corner of N. 22nd st. and E. Simmons ave. The empty lot is due east of this grocery store. Just south of this store is an apartment complex. In this apartment complex you already know of a few juveniles you have arrested for different types of crimes. This is a common drop off spot for stolen cars, so the exhausted juvenile's don't have to walk too far to get home after a night of crime.

Your midnight unit gets there to relieve you and you both walk up to the car from behind. A quick check around the inside, you see no one is around. The car is running and unlocked. You pop the truck open and check that too. No bodies in the trunk, good. (Always check this before your owner arrives)

Your back up takes over from here, you go home. Unless your department requires it, you have no paperwork to write, the relief unit does it.

First they run the tag on the car. The computer confirms it is stolen. You get the owners name and phone number. A quick check to make sure the car is drivable and has gas. The car's gas tank is on "Empty", otherwise it appears drivable. To save time, the owner is called first. The owner answers and she says she can come right away, she just needs to call her ride. She is told to bring gas and a Phillips screwdriver to turn the car on and off.

To begin processing the car, you check the position of the seat, it is all the way back. Someone very tall drove this car last. Turning on the car stereo it is set on a rap music channel and turned up all the way. Gas tank is on empty, probably just enough to get the bad guy home.

Next you dust for prints. Most surfaces on the car are porous or fibrous. Meaning not conducive to fingerprints. There is no need to dust these surfaces. Instead concentrate of the areas a person may naturally touch while operating a car. The door handles on the outside. Even though this is an area accessible to the public, if you get a print you could narrow down a search for a bad guy.

If you get a match on this car and the next car and the next car, and all the prints belong to the same person,,,your detectives will have a place to start.

Dust the inside glass, and the rear view mirror. Most people adjust this mirror to see. Sometimes they are dumb enough to leave a beautiful thumb print on the bottom edge of the glass for you.

Do a quick check of items in the car. Anything look unusual? A gun, ski mask, lots of cash laying around,,,no? just ordinary items? When the owner gets here you can confirm the things are actually hers.

Walk around the outside of the car. Any damage, bullet holes, signs it has been in an accident recently? Have your owner have a look around the outside too when she gets here.

You see the entire ignition cylinder has been ripped out and is lying on the driver's side floor. Outside the car, on the passenger's side there is a tiny indentation in the metal under the door handle. All this is common for the way the bad guy gets into the car. They like to get in by making the least amount of noise and obvious marks as possible.

Walk around the area around the car for any other evidence, items, anything that looks like it should not be there.

The owner gets there. You walk her around looking at the outside of the car, items inside the car and any damage. Everything seems like it is in place. No new damage. The car seat is way back for her and she listens to a jazz station all the time.

If your department allows, show her how to use the screwdriver to turn the car on and off through the glow ring, and fill up the tank with the gas can she brought.

Explain to the owner the car has a pick up on it showing it is stolen. You have already cancelled the pickup, but it may take a few minutes.

Give the owner a copy of the police report number so she can notify her insurance company and get her ignition fixed. You are done with her and she can take her car home now.

After she leaves, go to the apartment complex next door. There are a few apartments that face the field. Asking those residents you discovered no one saw a thing and they don't want to talk to police.

Special note: when you ran the tag on the car you received the information on your cars computer or from your dispatcher. You were notified that this car was stolen and reported to your agency yesterday. Hang onto this vehicle information, VIN number, year, make, model and owners information. We will need this to complete the report.

Synopsis

Unknown suspect(s) abandoned the listed vehicle, which had been previously reported stolen to this agency. The suspect(s) fled in an unknown direction. The vehicle was returned to the registered owner.

Police Report

Investigation:

I was assigned this call via computer dispatch to relieve midnight officer Smith. Smith located this abandoned vehicle while on routine patrol. On my arrival, I observed the listed vehicle, in a grassy field.

The vehicle was parked, with the engine still running on the east side of the grocery store. The vehicle was facing east toward the fence line.

The vehicle was checked for occupants, contraband, weapons or damages.

The vehicle seat was placed it its far rear position and the radio was set on 99.9FM. The vehicle's gas tank was on empty. The ignition cylinder was pulled out and a small hole was found under the passenger side door handle

I dusted the interior and exterior for fingerprints.

The vehicle was confirmed stolen on December 6, 2008 and was reported to this agency. The registered owner was contacted and did respond to take possession of her vehicle.

The immediate area, including the nearby apartment building was checked for suspects or witnesses, with negative results.

The pick up for the vehicle was cancelled through NCIC.

Police Report

Interview:

The complainant stated the vehicle has no new damages, other than the broken ignition cylinder and hole under the passenger side door. There are no items missing from the vehicle.

The complainant does not know anyone living or working in this area. She has no suspects in mind who could have taken her car.

She does wish to prosecute if anyone is arrested in connection with her car being stolen.

Interview:

Residents of Grey Oaks Apartments, Units 408, 410, 412 all faced the stolen vehicle. The occupants refused to speak to police, did not wish to get involved and refused to identify themselves.

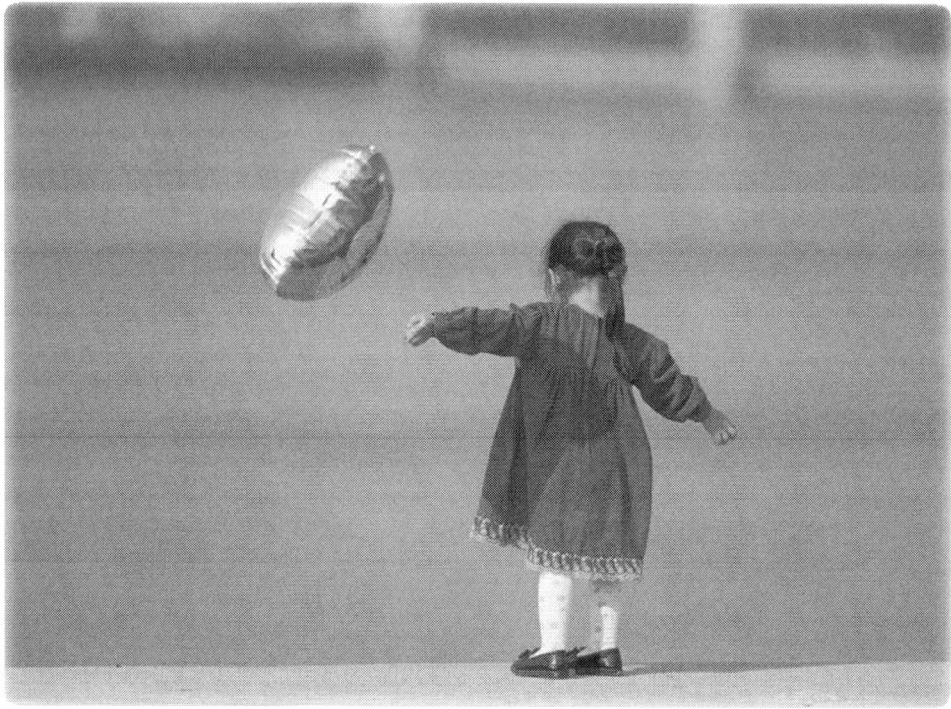

Missing Person

Your dispatcher sends you a call on your car's computer. A three year old child is missing. The child is a girl, she was in her back yard, playing and now the mother cannot find her. The child has been missing for about 30 minutes.

While you are driving to the call you ask the dispatcher to find out what the child looks like and what she was wearing. Your supervisor was already notified and you watch for any child matching her description, while you drive to the house.

The child's mother is there at the home when you arrive on the scene. First, you ask her if there is a swimming pool. She takes you to the back yard, the pool is clear and empty. Looking around the back yard, it is completely fenced in with a 6 foot, wood fence. The pool does have a child proof fence and the fence is up and in place.

There does not seem to be a way for the child to have gotten out of the yard, on her own. Next, you check the house. All the closets need to be checked, under the beds too. Kids can crawl into places to play hide and seek, but forget to tell mommy they are playing. They fall asleep and don't hear everyone calling for them.

While you are searching the house you are asking the mom for a more detailed description. This information is given out over the radio for other responding units. Those units are assigned to search the nearby homes. Back yard swimming pools first, then move out to yards, bushes, interviewing all neighbors as they go.

If you have a helicopter, have them fly over the area to look too. They will be flying at about 500 feet, so a clothing description with colors along with hair color will be most important to them.

Make sure your K-9 unit is responding too. Have the responding patrol units set up a perimeter about a block or so in each direction. The K-9 will begin from the child's home and follow the most recent scent. Try not to allow too many people in the scene and yard so the dog has less chance to follow a cop's scent around.

Your supervisor should be kept up on the missing child, search. So far we do not have any information about where the child is located. But, we do know where she is not. She is not in the house or immediate area.

Looking around, you see how it is very possible the child could have gone into the back door of her home, slipped past her mom and walked out the front door. There are no alarms or door chimes on the front door, just the rear door by the pool.

The child's father is on his way home from work. You call his employer back, after the dad has left and ask the employer where the dad was this morning. The dad's boss tells you the dad was at work the entire time and was caught by surprise when his wife called to say the child was missing.

We have several police officers on the scene, on foot looking for the child. So far we have no leads, but we do have enough to place an Amber Alert. Your supervisor needs to be notified so they can let your communications section know the criteria has been met. The Amber Alert needs to go out immediately.

The Amber Alert will contain the child's physical description only (suspect and vehicle description are not available) so it needs to be very detailed. You will want the child's age, height, weight, hair color, hair type, hair length, eye color. Does the child have any visible scars? Surgical scars, fall down scars? Birth marks, moles, freckles? Clothing, hats, shoes, hair ribbons, jewelry.

Does the child have any immediate medical needs? Scheduled medications? Physical limitations, mental limitations, is the child autistic? Has the child ever done this before? If so, where was she found the last time?

A photograph of the child needs to be obtained from the family. A current face shot and a couple of full body shots are what you will need. These photos can be reproduced to place with the report and if needed, given to local news stations for broadcast.

A few other things you will need to get from mom. Who is the child's dentist, doctor? We just need to know so we are being thorough. But, you know why we really need the dentist information. Just in case this search doesn't go so well.

Place the child in NCIC, (and your states system as well) then have the Amber Alert placed.

Your supervisor has notified you the Amber Alert has been placed. It is broadcasting right now on the highway signs, local news broadcasts, radio, cell phone and live internet streaming.

Individually you will want to interview the mom about any issues with the dad. Interview the dad about any issues with the mom. Unfortunately, most of these missing cases do involve a parent. Investigate this without accusing anyone of anything. All the immediate neighbors need to be interviewed as well.

The neighbors will need to be interviewed as to what they have seen over the last few days, including this morning and any known problems within the family. You will need contact information on every neighbor you talk to. Sometimes a statement means nothing today, but could be important later. If needed, this case will go to your detectives. The detectives will need to know who you spoke to the first day and what they had to say. If a neighbor is not at home, take down the address. Detectives may need to go back out in the evening to the address and speak to whoever lives there.

You just never know, the neighbor who was walking their dog, saw the dad move a carpet out of the house at midnight, drive off, and returned an hour later, could be significant information.

This is going to be considered an acute case. It will probably pull a lot of police officers out to start searching for the child on foot, immediately. Expect this search to get big, fairly quickly with lots of supervisors and detectives getting notified, and start showing up at your scene. Have very specific descriptions and information available to them when they arrive. Your agency may even set up a command post.

Remember to keep detailed notes on what you have done in this investigation. Do everything fast, notify everyone fast and get this search moving. You will need notes to show that you thought of everything, did everything and told everyone.

Unfortunately at this point it becomes a sit and wait for the family. Once the K-9 unit clears the perimeter of the house, the mom and dad can let their relatives in. Stay near this scene for questions and so you can overhear any comments, just in case. This is still a crime scene and you are still investigating, treat it as such.

When you finally do clear this scene, and tell the mom and dad you are leaving, units leave the perimeter and everyone drives off, it is no longer your crime scene. It returns to the mom and dad as a private residence. If you discover you need to go back in to retrieve anything, bedding, clothing you will most likely need to get a search warrant. Especially if it is looking like the parent(s), who live there may be involved.

This report will be documented on a basic incident report. Some states require the parents to sign an affidavit attesting to the fact they are the patents. Follow your department's requirements and get these forms signed prior to leaving. Then attach all these to your report.

Synopsis

The listed 3 year old female is missing due to unknown circumstances.

Police Report

Investigation:

I received this call via computer dispatch. On my arrival I met with and interviewed the complainant.

I observed the compl.'s home was a one-story brick home on the west side of the street facing east. The exterior of the home's rear yard was encircled by a 6' tall, wood privacy fence. The fence went to the ground and in most places was under the ground creating no openings. The gate for this fence was on the south side of the home. The gate was locked on the inside with a padlock that appeared to be rusted closed.

Inside the home I observed the closed off floor plan which placed the kitchen away from all doorways, and out of sight of the pool. The front door did not have an alarm or door chime. The rear door, leading out to the pool was standing open and had a door chime.

The rear yard had a pool which was very well maintained and clear. A child proof safety fence was in place and intact.

The appearance of the home was very well maintained and neat. The doors and windows were locked with no signs of forced entry or disturbances.

Police Report

Investigation: Cont.

The immediate area was searched for the child. The rear yard was searched, and the interior of the home, including all small spaces. The front yard, including the mother's vehicle were also searched, with negative results.

K-9 unit's responded and began a search of the exterior yard. (see supplement)

The helicopter responded and began an extended area search.

Detective White responded to the father's employer to conduct an investigation there. (see supplement)

Detective Jones researched the sexual predators in the area and responded to their residences. (see supplements)

Ofc.'s Bryant, Williams and Ryan responded and conducted a neighborhood search, home by home and interview neighbors. (see supplements)

I placed a pick up for the child with NCIC at 1100hrs.

Sergeant Riley was notified and placed an AMBER alert for the child at 1110hrs.

I received a recent photograph of the child and attached it to this report.

The complainant signed the parental affidavit for the missing child. The affidavit is attached.

Police Report

Interview:

The compl. stated she is the natural mother of the missing child. She stated she was home alone with the child. She opened the rear door to the back yard so her daughter could go out and play in her sandbox. The compl. then went into the kitchen. This was at approximately 1000hrs.

When the complainant went to check on her daughter about ten minutes later, the child was missing. The complainant said she checked the home, inside but could not find her and called police.

The complainant said she is not having any problems with the child's father and he would never remove or harm the child. the compl. is married to the child's father and they live together in this home. The complainant said she has no idea who would remove the child and she has no idea where he child could be. The child has never done this before.

The child does not have any acute medical conditions. She is not on any medications and has no injuries, scars or distinguishing marks.

The child's dentist is Dr. Smalley DDS. (223) 555-1212

The complainant cannot identify anyone who could be involved in the child being missing. The complainant will prosecute if anyone is arrested in connection with this offense.

Aggravated Assault

While driving near a bar in your zone you are stopped by several people running down the street toward your police car. You stop, and the people tell you there is a fight inside the bar.

You notify the dispatcher of the fight, give out the location and you and your partner go into the bar.

Once inside, you see the bar is almost full and there are two white males next to the pool table yelling at each other. The first man has his hands up in kind of a defensive stance. The second man has a pool stick over his shoulder like a baseball bat. The second man with the stick yells something and swings the stick at the first man's head.

The first man ducks down and just misses getting hit with the pool stick.

As the second man swings, someone in the crowd yells "cops!" and the man with the stick looks at you and drops the stick on the floor.

The second man immediately says he wasn't doing anything, they were just playing around. But, the first man says the second man tried to hit him because he is now dating the second man's ex girlfriend.

First, you grab the stick and hold onto it. You handcuff the man who was swinging the stick, for his own safety, and the safety of the others in the bar. Then you and your partner walk the two men out of the bar where you can see one another and hear what everyone is saying. You pat down both men for weapons and tell them they are not free to leave until you sort this incident out.

The rest of the patrons in the bar are fairly calm, cooperative and offer to speak to you if needed.

You begin by separating the two men so they cannot hear what is being said. The handcuffed subject is placed into the backseat of your police car and you check the other man, the victim for injuries.

This victim tells you he was never hit, but it was close and the handcuffed guy was chasing him all around the bar, threatening to kill him, when "the cops" came in.

When you ask why this all started the victim tells you he is now dating the handcuffed guys ex girlfriend. The handcuffed guy got drunk, didn't like seeing them together tonight and started yelling at them about an hour ago. The girlfriend left with her friends a short while ago. The victim was just about to leave when the handcuffed guy with the pool stick started chasing him around, swinging the stick.

The victim thinks the handcuffed guy was just so drunk he missed. The victim also thinks the handcuffed guy swung at him maybe three or four times, missing every time.

He does think the handcuffed guy did mean to hurt him. The victim was going to try to run out the door, but the handcuffed guy blocked him in the corner and swung again, right when the police showed up.

This is an important point. Make sure you ask: Did the bad guy say anything to the victim while he was swinging the stick? Just prior to swinging the stick? During the swing of the stick? On the follow through of swinging the stick?

The victim said the bad guy screamed, "I'm going to kill you, stay away from my girl".

And finally, ask this victim if he wishes to prosecute.

While you are interviewing the victim, your partner can interview the defendant. Remember, before you interview him you must remind him of his Miranda rights.

After he does agree to waive his rights and talk to him you ask him what happened. Now there are a couple of ways to go about this. This is technically an on-scene arrest that you did witness. You observed what happened, you do not need him to confess. You also do not need him to contradict, confuse or otherwise mess up your investigation. Me personally, I would not interview him. I saw what happened, off to jail you go. However, in the interest of completing the story here, we will interview him so we can see what his interview may look like written out on a police report.

During his interview with your partner the defendant told you he was just joking around and he had been drinking heavily. He said he was not really going to hit anyone, he just wanted to scare the victim. His demeanor right now was very apologetic and humble.

Next, we talked to a few people in the bar who were willing to talk to us and possibly testify. A couple sitting near the pool table saw the two men argue and the women with him leave quickly. The defendant was very loud and seemed to be trying to pick a fight with the victim. The victim seemed to be walking deeper into the bar with the defendant following. But, the victim kept watching his girlfriend as she and her friends ran out the door.

Once the girlfriend was out the door the victim started to leave as well. This is when the defendant picked up the pool stick and swung it at the victim. The victim was ducking to keep from being hit. The witnesses heard the defendant tell the victim he was going to kill him.

The witnesses said the defendant never actually hit the victim, but this was only because the victim kept ducking out of the way. The witnesses said this was definitely a real fight. They did not believe any of this fight was for show or playing around.

Synopsis

The defendant swung a pool stick at the victim, and missed. The defendant verbally threatened the victim. The defendant was arrested at the scene. There were no injuries

Police Report

Investigation:

I was advised of this offense by a passerby. While driving in front of the listed bar I was notified of a fight inside.

When I entered the bar I observed the defendant with a pool stick over his shoulder, holding it like a baseball bat. The defendant then swung the pool stick at the victim. While the defendant swung the pool stick he shouted at the victim.

I observed the victim duck, and was not struck. Individuals in the crowd shouted "police" and the defendant immediately dropped the pool stick on the ground.

I handcuffed the defendant and recovered the pool stick from the ground. Both the defendant and the victim were removed from the bar and taken outside.

Neither the defendant nor victim were injured.

I interviewed two witnesses regarding this offense.

I photographed the pool stick and returned it to the bar owner, the photo is downloaded to this report.

The defendant was delivered to booking.

Police Report

Investigation: Continued,

The defendant did have a strong smell of an alcoholic beverage on his breath. A BAC reading was taken when the defendant was delivered to jail. The BAC reading was 3.4, the reading is attached.

Interview: Defendant

The defendant waived his Miranda Rights and agreed to speak to police. The defendant stated he was just playing around and didn't even have a pool stick. The defendant said he does not know the victim.

Interview: Victim

The victim stated he is now dating the defendant's ex-girlfriend. The defendant saw them together tonight and started yelling at them. The victim stated his girlfriend got upset and left the bar.

Then the defendant picked up the pool stick and started chasing him around the bar, swinging the pool stick. The defendant told the victim, "I'm going to kill you, stay away from my girl".

The victim said the defendant kept chasing him and swinging the stick at him until the police arrived. The victim does believe the defendant meant to hit him with the pool stick.

The victim positively identified the defendant as the person who committed this offense. The victim does wish to prosecute.

Police Report

<u>Interview</u>: Witness #1

This witness stated they were in the bar for the entire incident. The witness observed the defendant chasing the victim around the bar with the pool stick. The witness did see the defendant swing the pool stick at the victim.

The witness does believe the only reason the defendant missed was due to the fact the victim kept ducking out of the way.

The victim did not hear any statements made by the defendant to the victim. The witness did hear the defendant yelling, but could not understand what was being said.

This witness positively identified the defendant as the person who committed this offense.

<u>Interview</u>: Witness #2

This witness stated they just walked into the bar and saw the defendant swing the pool stick at the victim's head. They saw the victim duck to avoid getting hit.

This witness did not see or hear anything else involving this incident.

The witness positively identified the defendant as the person who committed this offense.

And finally, the charging instrument needed to deliver the defendant to booking.

Charging Instrument

Probable Cause to prove crime:

The defendant did swing a pool stick at the victim's head, verbally threatening to kill the victim. The defendant missed the victim.

Identification of Defendant:

The Defendant was identified by the victim and witnesses as the person who committed this crime.

The defendant identified himself with a valid California driver's license.

Possession of Marijuana

Your zone includes a residential neighborhood. Burglaries have been a problem in the last few months, your sergeant has asked you to put yourself out there and walk around on foot. Just to see what you may come across.

You meet with your neighborhood crime watch resident, who allows you to hide your police car in their driveway, behind their house. While walking around, you and your partner watch for anything unusual in the neighborhood.

So far it is very quiet. The neighborhood is a historical, residential type area with a very heavy, tree canopy, with lots of landscaping and shrubbery. Walking between the houses you can see how it would be impossible for anyone from the street, or even a neighbor, to see each other's homes.

When you come around the corner you see a car on the road, in front of you, about a half a block away. The car is pulled over, the lights are off, but the engine is running. It looks like there are two people in the car. This car is between blocks. It is not directly in front of a home and it is not in front of a driveway. It is near the alleyway entrance that leads behind the homes.

After you notify the dispatcher of the car and its tag, it is not stolen, you watch it for a few minutes, un-observed. The two people in the car are sitting in the front seat. They seem to be waiting. There are no lights on in the interior and there is no music or radio noise. You can hear voices, but cannot tell what is being said.

Between them you see an orange glow. The driver is smoking. The driver then passes the cigarette to the passenger. It glows again as the passenger smokes too.

Since it has been about ten minutes and they only seem to be paying attention to themselves, you decide to approach their car. When you approach, you hear them talking and laughing. Then you smell the unmistakable odor of marijuana coming from the cars open windows.

The girl in the passenger seat hands the cigarette back to the driver, who smokes it again. You make yourselves known. The girl in the passenger seat screams, startled and jumps. The driver is calm and just looks at you. Your partner takes the cigarette from the driver's hand that is being held out the window. He was trying to hide it from you, but failed to see your partner, and almost handed the cigarette to him.

There is no one else in the car. You have both of the people exit the car. Asking them for identification, you ask where they currently live. The driver is not from the area. The girl lives nearby, and was getting a ride home from the driver. They work together at a local restaurant.

Both are extremely cooperative and seem a bit more embarrassed than anything.

Your partner tests the cigarette with a chemical reagent test. It does test positive for marijuana

Since both are adults, and they both have identification and they have ties to the community they can be released on their own recognizance. They can be given dates to appear in misdemeanor court.

Since we know we are going to "ROR" them, in most states we cannot search the vehicle they were in, unless the driver gives us permission.

We ask, and he allows us to search. We are looking for more marijuana, but anything goes here. No matter what we find, it becomes ours and we can charge accordingly. The driver can tell us to stop anytime, and we have to stop, but most people simply do not know this. He doesn't, and allows us a full search of his vehicle. We search and we come up empty. No other amount of marijuana is found, no other items or contraband is discovered.

When you begin to investigate drug crimes you can take a class to gain an in-depth knowledge with a state certification of drugs and how to recognize them. You will learn to investigate and testify about them in court. I highly recommend these courses. Your expertise in testifying in court is reduced to, "I am state certified in drug detection recognition". Your expertise is instantly recognized and you no longer have to qualify yourself to the judge, attorney or jury. But, if you need to qualify yourself, go with what you know and why you know these things.

Marijuana has a distinctive odor. I went to college parties where people were smoking marijuana. It is very distinctive, nothing smells like it. Even when you burn incense to try to cover it up, you can still smell the marijuana. When you see it in a bag it is recognizable even when the plant is dried up. The plant is dried and dries into a wadded up looking bunch of leaves. I have killed quite a few plants in my garden and nothing wads up quite like this. The smell is so distinctive and unusual. The distinctive odor is just that dramatic when you can smell and recognize marijuana. Testifying to this type of recognition in front of a jury is a method they can relate too.

Always conduct a chemical reagent test. You will need to testify to what made you think it was marijuana, then how you confirmed the substance was marijuana.

Follow your departmental guideline on arrests. My department allows a criminal affidavit, "Notice to Appear" to be completed and they get to leave without a physical arrest, no handcuffs, just sign the paperwork, take your copy and go home.

We complete the paperwork for each, have them sign, and put a thumbprint on the paperwork, place their arraignment date on it and they can leave. We keep what is left of the marijuana to place it into evidence for court.

At the end of your shift you return to the house where you hid your car. The neighborhood watch resident calls you over to ask you if you caught any burglars. You tell him no burglars tonight. Suddenly, behind him you see a familiar face. The girl you just arrested and released from the car is inside, behind him, trying to hide from you by melting into the wallpaper.

We witnessed this. No interviews, just a details report for an on-scene arrest.

Synopsis

The defendant's were observed smoking marijuana in the presence of the Affiant. Both were arrested and released on their own recognizance.

Police Report

Details:

While on foot patrol for burglary saturation, in the listed area I observed the defendant's sitting in a parked car. The car was parked next to an alleyway and was turned off.

Both occupants of the vehicle were seen passing a marijuana cigarette between them. Both were smoking from this same cigarette.

The vehicle had a very strong odor of marijuana coming from inside it.

Both defendant's were removed from the vehicle. The driver /owner of the vehicle gave police permission to search the vehicle for additional drugs or contraband, with negative results.

The marijuana cigarette tested positive with a chemical reagent test for marijuana.

The defendant's were arrested. Both qualified for Releasing on their own Recognizance.

Police Report

Details Continued,

Both received an affidavit with arraignment dates included. The defendant's thumbprints were placed on the affidavits.

The marijuana cigarette was photographed. The photos were downloaded into this report.

The marijuana cigarette was placed into evidence.

And the charging instrument used for the R.O.R. one for each defendant

Charging Instrument

Probable Cause to prove crime:

The defendant did smoke marijuana in the presence of police. Chemical reagent test was positive for marijuana.

Identification of Defendant:

This offense was witnessed by the Affiant. The defendant identified himself with a valid Indiana driver's license.

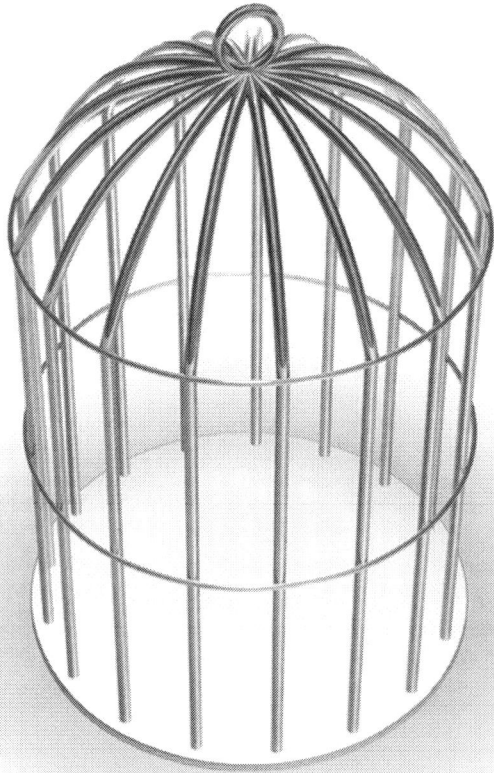

Petit Theft

The dispatcher notified you of a hysterical female complainant. The caller said someone has stolen her pet bird. The complainant thinks the suspect is nearby. The location the complainant is calling from is 506 East 10th street.

When you respond to the scene an elderly, white female is standing on her front porch screaming. You get out of your police car and walk toward her. While you are walking you notice the home the complainant is at is a one-story wood structure. The home faces north in the center of an average sized city lot, the home is on the south side of the street. The home is surrounded by a rusted chain link fence. The front gate is broken off of the hinges and missing. To the right (west) the lot is vacant with overgrown weeds. On the left (east) side of the complainants home there is another home, similar in appearance and condition. This home on the east side has several children approximately 10-12 years old running around in the yard.

As you get closer to the complainant you see she is standing on the front, covered porch of this home. She is standing next to a birdcage, which is empty. The complainant is crying hysterically and screaming at the neighboring children.

After several seconds of you trying to talk to her and calm her down she begins to tell you what has happened. She tells you she put her pet bird outside this morning, in his cage. When she went to check on the bird a few minutes ago the bird was missing.

She goes on to explain she thinks the neighbor kids took the bird and ate it. When you ask her why she thinks this she tells you the kids are always dirty, hungry and eat lots of chicken so they must have stolen the bird.

You look around the scene and ask for any other people in the home that may have seen what has happened. There is no one else in the home and this is the homeowner's home. She has lived here for 35 years. While you are looking around at the bird cage you notice the door to the cage is open. When you try to close the door it does close, but as soon as you take your hand away it swings open again, slowly.

As you remove your notepad from your pocket and begin to take the complainants personal information you also ask her the type of bird, color and the retail price of the bird.

The complainant tells you the bird is a blue parakeet and is invaluable. The bird is so smart it can sing the theme song to "cops". This alone makes the bird priceless, at least several thousand dollars.

Leaving the complainant on her front porch you walk around the home. As you circle the home you notice the back gate is closed securely, rusted shut with no openings anywhere.

Next you walk to the neighbor's house to speak with them. While you are talking to the group of kids their young mother comes outside to ask why their neighbor was screaming. When you explain the problem to this young mother, she smiles. This woman tells you the older woman is a bit off her rocker and screams a lot. None of the children are allowed to go into the elderly neighbor's yard for any reason, just to try to keep the peace. This young mother did not see anyone on the front porch and has not noticed the bird today, although putting the bird cage out every morning is a habit she watches the elderly neighbor do daily.

You explain to her that the cage door looks like it does not close properly, did the bird possibly just fly off?

The complainant is insistent that the children took her bird and ate it. She is demanding a report be filed.

After calming down the complainant more, you take all her information and search the immediate area for the bird.

Next you drive by the pet shop that is a couple of blocks away to check on the standard retail price of a blue parakeet.

Due to the broken cage door and lack of witnesses, we will reclassify this to a lost property report. Most agencies do require you to write a report for the complainant.

Synopsis

The complainant's pet parakeet is missing from its cage, which has a broken door.

Police Report

Investigation

I received this call via voice dispatch. On my arrival I met with and interviewed the complainant.

The complainant's home was a one story, wood frame home with a covered front porch. The entire home was surrounded by a chain link fence. The bird cage which had previously had the pet parakeet in it, was located on this covered porch.

The bird cage did appear to be broken. The door would not stay closed and seemed to be on crooked hinges which allowed the door to swing open on its own.

I interviewed the neighbor then searched the immediate areas, including shrubbery and trees for the missing bird.

The fair market value for the bid was determined by the "Flying Pets" pet shop.

Interview, Complainant

The complainant said she placed her bird cage outside this morning. When she went to check on the bird, the cage door was open and the bird was missing.

Police Report

Interview Continued,

The complainant thinks the neighbor children took the bird and ate it.

Interview Neighbor

This neighbor said she is familiar with the complainant's pet parakeet. The neighbor said she did not see anyone on the complainant's porch and her children are not allowed to even go into the complainant's yard.

Courtesy report.

Armed Robbery

Your dispatcher puts a call out on the radio of a robbery in progress. You know you are close and you start to drive in that direction. You notify the dispatcher of your location and make sure your supervisor was aware.

As you are driving in the direction of the call, it is a convenience store, the dispatcher gives you the description of the bad guy. You watch for anyone looking like the description, as you get closer. You park your car on the side of the store, out of the view of the inside, for safety.

You don't walk in the front of the store windows or drive past them. We are treating this as in-progress call, until **we** confirm it is not.

With your gun out, you approach the store from the side. The dispatcher holds down the air traffic for you. You can see the clerk on the phone. He is yelling into the phone and waving his arms around. There are no cars parked at the store parking lot. No one seems to be loitering around either. You tap on the glass so the store clerk can see you. He sees you and waves you inside. As you go in, you check the store quickly for any suspects, check for any injured people.

The clerk says the bad guy left only about a minute ago, running. The bad guy had a gun and ran out with money from the register. You confirm his description and re-send the description to the dispatcher for all the units on the street to look for. Especially the weapon information.

Since the crime has just occurred, there are no injuries and no other witnesses, we can continue the interview and begin our investigation. First, we need to control this crime scene. We need to get a few things done and we need the clerk to focus on what we need, for our investigation.

The best way to do this and keep people from coming in and messing up our fingerprints and other evidence, is to lock the store's door. This also keeps everyone inside, safe just in case the bad guy is still nearby and decides to return.

From here, we slow the complainant down just a bit and begin with the standard, what happened? We have the complainant walk us through the entire incident. Once he can walk us through the details, ask if he has ever seen this bad guy before. Regular customer, former employee, in earlier today, just looking around? Can he possibly recognize this bad guy if he sees him again?

Was the bad guy alone? Did he drive off or was there someone else driving. Have the clerk describe what was going on when he first noticed something was wrong. Did he notice a car parked at a funny angle outside. A car driving past several times. A person coming in and out but not buying anything?

The clerk may have noticed these things, but did not raise an alarm with him at the time.

The clerk tells you he does think he saw this guy earlier in the day. It was about the time school got out, so the store was packed. But, the clerk remembers him because he was a bit old to be in school. He loitered around just like the high school kids do, but he wasn't really taking to any of them.

The clerk remembered this guy had a black hoodie on it with gold graphic print that was in a busy design. He had a goatee type beard, looked a bit older than the high school kids, maybe early twenties or so. The bad guy was about your height and build. (You are 5,10" and around 170). He was a very dark skinned black male. No glasses or anything else out of the ordinary about him. He seemed to move, walk and talk just fine. The gun was definitely in his right hand.

When he came in he was very fast, direct and came right to the register. He held the gun at a funny sideways angle, like on TV. And said, "Money now!". He stared right at the clerk and didn't even look around.

When the clerk handed him the money, the bad guy stuffed it into the front pocket of his hoodie and ran out the door. When he ran out, he ran to the right. The clerk didn't hear or see any car, so he is not sure if the bad guy ran off, or got into one a bit down the roadway.

The clerk remembers the gun was a black metal. Not the kind with the round barrel, but the one that looks flat and square. There is a great face shot of the bad guy on the security system. We can look at it and send it to our departmental email account.

Take down detailed information on what was taken, weapon type and bad guys description including any vehicles. Check the immediate area, businesses, homes for any witnesses.

Once you are comfortable you have the details of before, during and after this crime, begin processing the scene. Many stores have the vertical measuring tape along the door frame. The purpose of this is for the clerk to look at this as the bad guy runs out to tell what height he is. Useless. I never had a clerk do this for me, ever. Don't waste time on this. Dust the scene for prints in areas where the bad guy actually touched. Since there is a surveillance system, we are having the clerk send a copy to your departmental email. Separate a single frame of any upper torso shots individually. These can be enhanced later.

We placed another alert on the police radio with the latest description, time and direction of travel.

Go around the store and look for guns thrown down, clothing he stripped off as he ran, or money accidentally dropped. Also, check with the homeless guys sleeping at back to find out what they saw.

Once you are done with the scene, the clerk is calmed back down you can let them open it up for business again and we get to start on the report.

Taking money, or anything of value by force, threat of force or intimidation all fits the requirements of armed robbery just about everywhere.

Synopsis

An unknown black male suspect pointed a gun at the victim/clerk, took cash from the listed business and fled on foot south from the store.

Police Report

Investigation

I received this call as a BOLO from computer dispatch. I was on patrol less than 8 blocks away and immediately responded to the scene. On my arrival I met with and interviewed the complainant/ clerk.

I observed the business was the Quiki-Mart, located on the west side of the street, facing east toward N. Meridian Ave. The business parking lot had no cars in it on my arrival. There were no individuals in the area, or in the store.

The business had all the lights on both inside and out in the parking lot. The store had an entire glass window front, but the view from the street was obscured by numerous posters and signs on the glass.

A more detailed description and direction of travel was obtained and placed on the radio again for responding units. Sgt. Mills was advised of the offense.

I processed the scene for fingerprints, they are attached to this report.

A digital surveillance video of the offense was recorded by the store's cameras. The offense was downloaded and is attached to this report. A single face frame was also separated and is attached to this report.

Police Report

Investigation: Continued

After processing the crime scene, I searched the area around the store for any additional evidence or witnesses. I met with and interviewed a witness that is homeless and lives behind this convenience store.

No additional evidence or information was obtained.

Interview: Complainant

The complainant stated he was working alone in the store tonight when a black male came in, walked directly toward the register and pointed a gun at him.

The B/M suspect said, "money now". The complainant handed all the money in the register to the suspect. The suspect ran out the door and to the right, on foot.

The suspect was very direct when he came in and went directly toward the register, without stopping or looking around. The suspect pointed the gun sideways at the complainant. The gun was a black, semi-automatic handgun of unknown caliber.

The suspect was wearing a black, hoodie type sweatshirt that he had pulled around his face, partially concealing himself. The complainant said the suspect held the gun in his right hand. The suspect had a gotee type beard. The suspect walked and talked normally, no other distinguishing marks or features were noted.

The complainant does believe the suspect was in the store earlier. At approximately 1500 hrs when school was getting out and the store was very crowded. He does not believe the suspect purchase anything, but the suspect was loitering around with the crowd of high school students.

The complainant does believe he can recognize the suspect if he sees him again. The complainant was not injured during this offense.

The complainant and the corporate office do wish to prosecute.

Police Report

Interview: Witness

This witness stated he lives at the back of the convenience store, behind the dumpster. He stated he did see a B/M running by a bit ago, but didn't think anything about it. He said the B/M was wearing a black jogging suit and ran west on W. Dunham Ave.

The witness stated he can recognize the suspect if he sees him again.

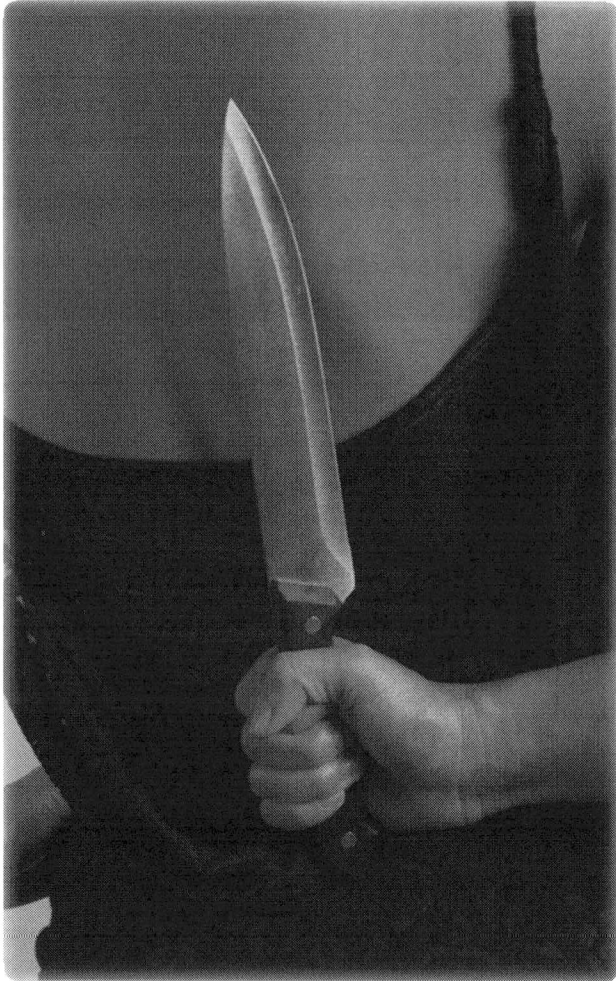

Your dispatcher gives you a 911 call of a possible fight. The dispatcher heard a female screaming over the phone, then the line went dead. There is no answer on the call back.

When you pull up to the house, you park about 2-3 houses away. When you get out, you get out quietly and walk in the direction of the home. The area is quiet, no sounds, no fighting. Knocking on the door, you look inside the home through the open curtains, everything is quiet. A female answers the door.

The female tells you to come in. Stopping first, you ask her if there was a fight here. She says yes but "he" is next door. She is holding an ice pack to her face.

Asking her if she needs medical attention, she says yes. She said she was hit and is feeling dizzy. You call for an ambulance for her and ask her what happened. She is crying, raising her voice and still seems very upset. She tells you that her husband is crazy and hit her for no reason.

You can smell alcohol on her breath, not only when she speaks, but around her. She seems very drunk. You get a chair for her so she does not fall down and hurt herself further. Asking her again, what happened, she says her husband came home drunk, started yelling at her and punched her in the mouth. When you ask where he is, she says next door . Why is he next door? She tells you that is where they live, this is the neighbor's home. She called 911 from here.

When you ask where the fight happened, she says, next door at home. She says he needs to go to jail, he is drunk and loves to fight with police. He is abusive to his kids, on medication and doesn't have a job.

Before you leave the house to go next door, you ask her if there are any weapons in the home? She said nothing but regular kitchen knives. Asking her if there are any other people in the house, she says his two sons are in the home with him.

Looking at her injuries, she has a swollen lip and is bleeding from her mouth or gums. She is showing you a tooth that was knocked loose as well. Except for the dizziness, she said she has no other injuries, he only hit her one time, with his fist.

Now, in most states all you need for an arrest is probable cause. She has given us plenty of probable cause to arrest her husband for battery, domestic violence. But, when someone says, "for no reason", there is usually a reason. And there are always two sides to every story. I want to get both sides, make sure they match up before I finish making my decision on what happened here.

Once the ambulance arrives and starts attending to her, we go next door to find the husband. When we walk next door, he is outside, sitting on the front porch. He says, "I guess you are looking for me, huh?". Then he stands up. He is about 6,5" pretty big build. We had him sit back down, so we can talk. Yikes, very big guy. He immediately sat back down. He seemed very calm, a bit nervous. But, not in an aggressive manner.

I start by asking him if he was ok. He says sure, "it didn't hit me". What? What didn't hit him, his own fist? Ok, what happened here?

He says he was just coming home from work when he saw his wife puling into the driveway just behind him. She was swerving and almost rolled into his truck. She got out of her car and he could tell she was drunk. She started yelling at him and told him she was out looking for him. He told her she should have checked his work, that is where she can find him during work hours. This made her mad and she shoved past him to run into the house.

When she is drunk, which is often he does not like to argue with her. When he walked in she had the cordless phone in her hand. She said she was calling the police to have him arrested. When he said why, she told him because she wanted him out of the house for the night. He tried to take the phone from her so he could talk to the dispatcher himself, but she yanked it back. There was a pulling fight over the phone. She pulled so hard, while she was screaming, he just let go.

She pulled back so hard the phone hit her in the mouth. She screamed and threw the phone at him. He ducked, and the phone missed. It went somewhere behind the couch. Then she ran at him, scratched his face with her fingernails and ran out the door. He had two sets of scratches on each side of his face.

He said he later found her car keys, dropped them into his pocket, so she wouldn't drive. He assumed she ran to the neighbor's house, so he sat down to wait on the police.

When we went into the home he showed us the dent in the wall where the phone hit. The phone was still laying on the floor behind the couch.

We then talked to his two sons. They said their stepmom is drunk a lot and likes to pick fights. They just try to ignore her and stay out of her way.

We separate them to ask them what happened here. Both of the boys said the same thing. She came in yelling, tugging the phone. Their dad let go and the phone hit her. She clawed their dad's face and she ran out. Both of the boys saw the entire incident.

The husband does not want to prosecute. The wife does.

Now in most states the participants do not have the option to decline prosecution in domestic violence cases. If you call for police and give us probable cause to arrest, someone has to go to jail. But, who goes to jail here?

Synopsis

The defendant scratched her husband's face during an argument. The defendant was arrested at the scene.

Police Report

Investigation:

I was given this call via voice dispatch of a 911 call with a female caller yelling in the background. There was no answer on the call back.

On my arrival at 1434 W. Chester, I met with and interviewed the defendant.

The defendant had visible injuries to her face. She had a bloody lip and a loose tooth. She complained of dizziness and was treated by an ambulance. Fire Rescue Unit #14 responded. The defendant refused to be transported to the hospital.

The defendant then directed us next door, 1436 W. Chester, to the location of the offense.

At this location we met with and interviewed the complainant. The complainant had several scratches approximately 4" long, on his face in the pattern of fingernails. The complainant refused medical attention.

This residence was a one story, block home on the west side of the street. Inside the home I observed a dent on the west, living room wall. This dent was approximately 4 feet up from the floor and was about 6" in diameter. A cordless phone was located on the floor, directly under the dent.

There were no other damages or signs of a disturbance in the home.

I then met with and interviewed the complainant's children separately.

Police Report

Investigation: Continued

I took several photographs of the complainant's face, the dent on the wall and the defendant's face as well. The photographs were downloaded to this report as an attachment.

After the interviews were completed I responded back to the defendant at the neighbor's home and placed her under arrest.

The defendant was delivered to booking where the jail required her BAC reading. The defendant's BAC was 2.8, the reading is attached.

Interview: Defendant

The defendant said she was out looking for her husband, the complainant tonight because he is out with another woman. She said she could not find him so she came home. When she pulled into their driveway she saw him there first and went to confront him.

She said he hit her with his fist, on her mouth for no reason so she tried to call the police. She said he took the phone from her and threw it at the wall. The defendant then ran to the neighbor and called 911.

The defendant said she has no idea how his face got scratched.

The defendant refused to be transported the hospital.

Interview: Complainant

The complainant said he was pulling into the driveway of his home when his wife, the defendant pulled in behind him. The complainant said he knew instantly she was intoxicated by the way she was screaming incoherently at him.

The complainant walked her into the home to try to talk to her but she

Police Report

Interview: Continued

continued to scream at him, so he walked away from her. The defendant told him she was going to call the police and have him arrested, so he would be out of the house.

The complainant said he did try to take the phone away from her at that point, but when she began pulling so hard he just gave up and let go. She pulled the phone back so hard she smacked herself in the mouth with the phone. Then the defendant threw the phone at him, missed and hit the wall with it.

The defendant then ran up to him and scratched his face with her fingernails. The complainant pushed her away from him and the defendant ran out the door.

The complainant refused medical attention.

The complainant does not wish to prosecute.

Interview: Witness #1

This witness, the complainant's son stated he saw the defendant grab the phone and try to pull it away from his dad. He said his dad let go and the defendant hit herself in the mouth. The defendant then scratched his dad's face.

The defendant was screaming the entire time threatening to call the police and have the complainant arrested.

The defendant is this witnesses step-mother.

Interview: Witness #2

This witness, the complainant's son stated his stepmom is often intoxicated and yelling at his dad. The defendant did hit herself with the phone then try to hit is dad with it. The defendant then scratched the complainant and ran off.

<u>Charging Instrument</u>

<u>Probable Cause to prove crime:</u>

The defendant did scratch the complainant's face (her husband) with her fingernails.

<u>Identification of Defendant:</u>

The Defendant was identified by the complainant and witnesses as the person who committed this crime.

The defendant identified herself with a valid California driver's license.

Index

C

D

E

F

G

H

I

J

K

L

M

T

U

V

W

Resources

Some of the content in this book I made up, the rest I looked up, here is where I got my information:

AMBER Alert Program, 2003 , Department of Justice

    http://www.amberalert.gov/guidelines.htm

Frank, Thomas, USA today: Face recognition next in terror fight,

    Retrieved on December 28, 2008 from,

    http://www.usatoday.com/news/washington/2007-05-10-facial-

    recognition-terrorism_N.htm

Federal Bureau of Investigation, U.s. department of justice, Retrieved on

    December, 11, 2008, from, http://www.fbi.gov/ucr/ucr.htm

How to really, really write those boring police reports, Clark, K. K.,

    2006, Loose Leaf Law Publications, Flushing NY

Humphreys, P. , 2008, Video surveillance on public streets: A new law

    enforcement tool for local governments, Retrieved November

    2008, http://www.nysba.org/AM/Template.cfm?Section=Home&CONT

    ENTID=18214&TEMPLATE=/CM/ContentDisplay.cfm

Jacob. K. , 1991 A guide to police writing, Carsel, Canada

Kirzner & Mandell , 2003 The holt handbook

    Heinle & Heinle, Florence, KY

The language of law: dictionary and research guide, Retrieved on

    December 12, 2008 from: http://www.123exp-law.com/t/03784078530/

Reis, George, 2004 Admissibility in court, Evidence Technology

Magazine, Retrieved on December 24, 2008 from:

    http://www.imagingforensics.com/admissibilityincourt.pdf

Wood, J. Federal judicial center, Federal courts Retrieved Nov, 2008

    http://www.fjc.gov/public/pdf.nsf/lookup/cvra0806.pdf/$file/cvra0

    806.pdf

Photography, BigStockPhotography.com

Printed in Great Britain
by Amazon